MW00883432

HEAVEN'S LANGUAGE

Revelation: One Nugget at a Time

Reuben Hostetler

Unless otherwise indicated, all Scripture quotations are from The ESV® Bible (The Holy Bible, English Standard Version®), © 2001 by Crossway, a publishing ministry of Good News Publishers. Used by permission. All rights reserved.

Scripture quotations marked (TPT) are from The Passion Translation®. Copyright © 2017, 2018, 2020 by Passion & Fire Ministries, Inc. Used by permission. All rights reserved. ThePassionTranslation.com.

Scripture quotations marked (NIV) are taken from the Holy Bible, New International Version®. Copyright © 1973, 1978, 1984, 2011 by Biblica, Inc.™ Used by permission of Zondervan. All rights reserved worldwide. www.zondervan.com. The "NIV" and "New International Version" are trademarks registered in the United States Patent and Trademark Office by Biblica, Inc.™

Scriptures marked (NKJV) are taken from the NEW KING JAMES VERSION (NKJV): Scripture taken from the NEW KING JAMES VERSION®. Copyright© 1982 by Thomas Nelson, Inc. Used by permission. All rights reserved.

Scripture quotations marked (CSB) have been taken from the Christian Standard Bible®, Copyright © 2017 by Holman Bible Publishers. Used by permission. Christian Standard Bible® and CSB® are federally registered trademarks of Holman Bible Publishers.

Scripture quotations taken from the (NASB®) New American Standard Bible®, Copyright © 1960, 1971, 1977, 1995, 2020 by The Lockman Foundation. Used by permission. All rights reserved. lockman.org

Scripture quotations marked (NLT) are taken from the Holy Bible, New Living Translation, copyright ©1996, 2004, 2015 by Tyndale House Foundation. Used by permission of Tyndale House Publishers, Carol Stream, Illinois 60188. All rights reserved.

Scripture quotations marked (AP) are the author's paraphrase.
Scripture quotations marked (KJV) are from the King James Version, public domain.

Cover Design: Arlen Miller

Copyright © 2024 Reuben Hostetler. All Rights Reserved.

To order books, contact the author at reunettt@gmail.com.

ISBN: 9798342903332

Contents

Acknowledgments

A thank you to all those who have walked beside me and spoken truth into my life.

Below are a few who made this book possible.

To my wife, Nettie, for your outstanding servant's heart and your unwavering support. You are the most unselfish person I know. You tend to forget about yourself for the sake of others.

To Arlen Miller, for book cover design. It was a pleasure working with you. You did a phenomenal job.

To Elaine Starner, you did a phenomenal job at everything from editing to proofreading to interior layout. Thank you for your patience and skill.

Introduction

Over the years, the Lord has been faithful. He keeps speaking and changing us from the inside out. His mercy is new every morning. Just when we start to think we are drying up, when we think it's over, God says, "This is where my work begins!" He meets us wherever we are and speaks words of life that go deep down inside and change us so that we are no longer the same person.

Whatever life brings your way, make sure that Christ is the foundation you are laying. He is the only foundation that will stand the test of time and take you all the way through life and into eternity; He is the only foundation where condemnation is unable to touch your soul. Life is too short to live for a short-term goal, working to reap a carnal reward only to lose our soul at the end.

This book comes forth from years of seeking God and His answers in prayer. In the natural, it looked like there was no answer; when in reality, God was making and developing character and maturity through testing. Later in life, I would learn that God chastens those he loves.

We have our own ideas of where we want to go in life, but God's ways are always higher and better. Moses spent 40 years in the desert being prepared by God for His life mission. Jesus was at the age of 30 before His ministry began. So it is with us; if we are ever to be used by God, there will always be a time of preparation.

I made the decision to write this book when the thought kept coming to my mind: *Why should I receive what God speaks and then keep it to myself?* We should never be people who hold back when we have the opportunity to bless those around us. Fresh water does not stay fresh if it does not keep moving. My goal and hope in writing is that somehow the very presence of God will be felt by those who read and the heart of Christ will come through and show those who need God's touch that there is hope and life in who Christ is.

When we set our hearts to understand His Word with our all, revelation finds its way into our everyday circumstances. If you find the book to be a blessing, then take a moment to thank the One who gave His life for the souls of all mankind, Jesus Christ.

Reuben Hostetler

I am the LORD; that is my name;
my glory I give to no other,
nor my praise to carved idols.
(Isaiah 42:8)

1 THE GLORY OF GOD OR MAN?

We live in a world of comparison and competition. We are tempted every day to desire the glory that comes from man. Man has a lot to offer when it comes to praise, prosperity, and feeling accepted, and we desire approval from man. And yet, God says, "My glory does not come that way."

What about God's glory? What about seeking His Kingdom first?

I believe many times the reason we don't desire His Kingdom and what God has to offer is because of our nearsighted natural man. When we become nearsighted and begin to look for approval from our fellow man, the glory of God is held back. If we instead see ourselves as set apart for God and set our hearts on seeking that which can't be seen with our natural eyes, God opens up a realm that the natural man cannot see. The glory of God will give us more than we can even begin to imagine!

The Bible says the Kingdom of Heaven is like a grain of mustard seed sown in a field. "It is the smallest of all seeds, but when it has grown, it is larger than all the garden plants and becomes a tree, so that the birds of the air come and make nests in its branches" (Matthew 13:31-32).

Our natural man does not desire the smallest or the least, but many times what we fail to understand is how much power is in the least of the seeds of the Kingdom. Christ provided salvation for the whole world, but He did it through surrender and not self-gratification. He counted His life as nothing and became the Savior of the world.

2 IDENTITY AND INTIMACY

The first sin that Adam and Eve were tempted with in the garden was the temptation to think God would not fight for them and God did not have their best interest in mind. I believe the main reason they reached for the fruit was because they thought they needed to take matters into their own hands. If we don't believe that God is fighting for us and that He will fight for *me* as well as anybody else, we start engaging in unhealthy relationships.

Another example is Cain and Abel. Cain believed that God was fighting for Abel but did not accept Cain's own sacrifice. To this day, those two races of people have that same issue between them. But the moment they both turn to Christ and believe Christ is fighting for both of them, walls begin to crumble and relationships are restored.

As humans, we are tempted to have many ranks of people who are important, and we place people on heights where only Christ belongs. The problem with this is that it can trap us in thinking that God would not fight for me, and from this mindset, many unnecessary sins are birthed. Whether the sin is unforgiveness, bitterness, resentment, immorality (and the list goes on), I believe most spring from the same root. If we don't believe God is on our side, we end up in all kinds of dark sins and struggles, fighting for ourselves.

Many problems would be solved if we would only believe that God is on our side.

The reason Jesus came to earth was to prove that we are not left alone and to deal with our sin of separation from God. He is fighting for us and has won the battle. What more do we need?

How could Christ ever prove His acceptance of us more than by what He did on the cross? His death was for the people who killed Him. One of His last cries was, "Father, forgive them; they don't know what they're doing!" He had a cry coming from His heart for those who crucified Him. How His heart must have ached as He gave His all to prove He is fighting for us.

Only when we come to an understanding of our acceptance by the Father can we say with the words in the Bible, "If God is for us, who can be against us?" (Romans 8:31).

If there will be any intimacy with Christ, there must first come a time when our identity issues are settled and we are convinced that God loves all mankind, including ourselves. The question is, can I accept the fact that Christ fought for me as much as He did for anybody else? And that He fights for me *now*?

Many problems would be solved if we would only believe that God is on our side.

If we don't understand how we can possibly forgive things done against us by others, it is simply because we don't understand how much we have been forgiven and are now accepted. Christ fights for me just as much as He fights for anybody else! The moment we accept this fact, we become unshakable and resentment and unforgiveness become useless sins.

For the first time in life, we say, "Why would I not forgive, when I myself have been forgiven so much and Christ is fighting for me?"

3 SOARING WITH THE EAGLES

In today's world, there are many opinions on what true success is. Success can never be measured by money alone. In the Bible, many wicked kings ruled and suppressed the people and yet were wealthy. The world's gauge of success should never be the Christian's gauge of success! If what I have has been gained by killing others, could that be true success? Or could it be that it's only the result of greed? Yet we call it God's blessing!

One of the greatest tests that will ever come to a person is the one of being mistreated and still having the ability to treat people the way Jesus treated the people who hung Him on a tree. The further we go in the Christian life, the more we learn not to respond out of our feelings and things that come against us from other people. I believe one of the things that came as a result of Solomon asking God for wisdom was that he could bring people together when others only got agitated by the problems they saw in people.

Our response to conflict and those who oppose us tells how much of Christ lives in us. The only true measure of success is the life of the One who was willing to die in order to bring life to others.

4 A HEART OF YES

And I heard the voice of the LORD saying, "Whom shall I send, and who will go for us?" Then I said, "Here I am ! Send me." (Isaiah 6:8)

Our Creator knows whether we are waiting to hear His voice so we can say yes with anticipation and excitement or if we are of those who would rather say no to everything He speaks.

Next-level Christianity is always yes when God speaks, rather than "Well, I'm not sure that I can or want to." A no to God is always associated with resistance and an unwillingness to move forward.

Why would a man find pleasure in always holding back and saying no? There is no life in holding back and always staying the same. This can be seen in many strong religious cultures in which staying the same and never changing is looked at as the right way to live. But whether it is personal habits or religious culture or business practices, staying the same is a sure sign that there is no proper growth!

I believe one of the reasons people say no is because they are afraid of losing control, but what we fail to recognize is that we are not in control regardless if we hold back or let go. Wisdom tells the pilot to use his throttle on a plane or he will lose his flight. Holding back and saying no will take you down!

A Bible story we're all familiar with is the story of Zacchaeus. Jesus found a heart of yes when He met Zacchaeus. Even though the Bible says this tax collector was a wealthy man, he found something fascinating about the Person who created the entire universe. As a result of his yes, salvation came to his house.

The moment Zacchaeus sought after Jesus more than his daily occupation and put in the special effort to do something out of the ordinary to get just one glimpse of Jesus, he got the attention of the Messiah. Everyone around him still saw him as a tax collector out to hurt people. What they did not see was a heart that was bending to the Creator of the universe. His heart was broken to the point that he gave up the things he had gotten by his own power. True repentance had entered Zacchaeus's heart.

The whole point of Christianity is that we yield our lives to Christ and no longer do life our way. We yield all control to the Holy Spirit, and He decides how to run our life.

Those who have a heart that is always ready to give a yes whenever God speaks are guaranteed to move forward in life.

- - - - -

One of the enemy's tactics is to use our flesh to influence us to take matters into our own hands. He wants believers to go back to a life of rebellion where they no longer trust God. Rebellion is as serious as the sin of witchcraft (1 Samuel 15:23); both attempt to take control that belongs to God. Trying to take charge of my own life is rebellion. And whenever we see extreme attempts to control, we have to wonder if there is a deep underlying root of witchcraft.

Don't think for a moment that because you belong to a Spirit-led body of Christ or a "good" family that you won't be tempted to take matters into your own hands. Human nature loves to be in charge, and you must be aware of this.

The Holy Spirit has no place to operate in the life of the one who needs to call the shots. If we yield to the Holy Spirit, we give Him the right to guide our life, and we can trust that we will never be left alone. The Holy Spirit is our everything, our best friend, our guide, our transforming power.

When our lives are totally yielded to Christ, we do not want to be in control but love to be fully committed to the Creator of the universe. We simply don't have time to control life. Life is too short for us to be doing our own thing!

To offer our life as a daily sacrifice is to learn to let Christ be the One who gives us the mission He has for us. How can we have a yes for God if we are still in charge of our own life?

5 EMPTY AND VOID WITHOUT FORM

Do you find your life empty and void, without form? If so, this is exactly the condition of the earth before the universe was formed. The Bible says it was empty and void, without form, absolutely nothing.

There is something about *zero* or *nothing* or *empty* that the Lord takes pleasure in!

Many times we have something we hold on to, and it keeps God from working because we hold on to the little bit we have.

But when we find ourselves in a place of absolute nothing, it's a good place for the Holy Spirit to step in and transform our life. *Zero* is no threat to our Lord! When our life has zero balance and we feel like there's nothing to give, this becomes the perfect situation for the miraculous power of Heaven to do a marvelous work.

> *Jesus said, "Those who are well have no need of a physician, but those who are sick. I came not to call the righteous, but sinners." (Mark 2:17)*

In Matthew 19:23, Jesus told His disciples that those who are rich have a hard time entering into the Kingdom. The Bible says many who are first will be last, and the last first. And the one who wants to buy the pearl must sell everything he has to buy it.

It's humanity to think, *If I can make it on my own, why should I turn to a higher source?* The truth is, we all have a desperate need—we are empty and void. If only we can recognize how great our need is! The enemy blinds us by convincing us that we can do life on our own. In reality, that is a lie. We desperately need to see how much we need Him.

The way the Christian advances should not be the same way the world advances. The system of this world speaks this: "I gain by cutting off those who are my competitors." Not so in the teachings of Jesus. We are told to bless those who curse us and pray for those who despitefully use us. The whole point is that we don't depend on our strengths but we look to Christ, from whence comes our help.

The gospel is this: When we surrender to God, He begins to fight for us and takes us farther than we could ever go on our own! I believe many who are last will be first because they allow Heaven to fight for them.

But the one who fights for himself is the one who will end up last because he is fighting his own battle, and the ability that he has is the only thing that is for him. Who are we looking to for help? Is it still our own strength, or are we looking to the One who knows how to fight our battle?

It takes many zeros to make a million. Unless you count your life as nothing, God will never put a 1 (Christ) in front of all your zeroes!

6 CALLED OUT, SET APART

As saved people, we are called out, set apart, and unable to connect with the mindset of this world.

Or are we? Does our path look different from the paths taken by those who have never experienced salvation? Or are we "slightly" saved, living with the same passions as those who don't know Christ?

The questions need to be asked: Are we set apart? Is our heart after Him, to the point that we see Him and desire Him so much that we can say with Paul, "To live is Christ, and to die is gain"?

The closer we get to Him, the more we lose our desire for the carnal things life has to offer. If we walk in a place where His glory consumes our lives, the challenge to stay passionate about life on earth can be difficult at times. Unless we are filled with the desire to do His will, we will lose our purpose for being here on earth.

The path of the believer can be a lonely path, and at times we need to remind ourselves why we are here and say with Paul, "To live is Christ, and to die is gain!"

In this life, we face many dark and lonely valleys, and at times we wonder, *Is this the last one? Will I make it? Will I spend the rest of my life like a dried-up plant without hope?*

But as we learn to trust His Spirit, we know He is faithful. When the Holy Spirit comes, His presence fills our mind and inspiration fills our soul and new life springs forth! Courage begins to flow like a steady stream into our soul. The Spirit of Christ is a Being of hope and inspiration, and our minds can't help but find hope, when only a moment before we were wondering how to take the next step.

Jesus wasn't afraid to spend His entire life on earth for the soul of man. He took upon Himself the thing that was destroying humanity. He died a dark, lonely death for you and for me.

How this should increase our desire to have a relationship with Christ! Especially the glorified Christ, who in Revelation is seen as the one with eyes like flames of fire, hair white as wool, and feet like polished bronze.

In John 14:21, Jesus says, "And he who loves me will be loved by my Father, and I will love him and manifest myself to him."

If He spent everything for me, how much can I spend for Him?

7 FROM BEGGAR TO SON

In the parable of the son who took his inheritance and wasted it, the son remembered that his father was a good father and he never had lack. The son knew his father would have plenty of resources; he always had plenty.

The heart of the father was to bring complete restoration, oneness with his son restored. He said, "Go get the best robe, my own robe! Put on him the ring, the seal of sonship, and bring the best shoes!"

Our Father's heart is to always give and not hold back. His giving transforms the way we think and the way we act. His giving will change how we look at life. Nothing can stay the same in His Kingdom.

We find ourselves tending to hold back, but our Father doesn't think that way. He is a master giver. He can't hold back; He gives life like no other! In the life of Jesus, when a person asked for healing, Jesus could not hold back; giving was who He was and still is today.

If humanity could only understand that the way of salvation is open. The veil in the temple was torn. The reason He hung on a cross was to show how willing He was to give. If we ask, we receive!

8 A CRY IN THE MIDST OF BATTLE

In the Psalms chapter 77, the writer finds himself in a place where his soul refuses to be comforted. His spirit faints. He says, "I am so troubled that I cannot speak!" (v. 4). He asks if the Lord will spurn him forever and never again be favorable toward him. "Has his steadfast love forever ceased?" (v. 8).

We are no different. The psalm speaks of people in battle and we are people in battle. The question is, do we recognize our only way "out" is finding our Master in the midst of it all?

Later in the same chapter, the psalmist writes, "Then I said, 'I will appeal to this, to the years of the right hand of the Most High.' I will remember your wonders of old. I will ponder all your work, and meditate on your mighty deeds!" (vv. 10-12).

As our life as a Christian keeps growing, we come to recognize it's not a question of *will we* face times of questioning or *why* do I find myself in a valley or pit. The question is, *how long* will I stay there? Can I stand up the next day and keep my eyes on Christ and allow His strength to flood my soul?

The enemy of our souls wants us to lose focus and allow yesterday's defeats to keep us in bondage; but the Bible reminds us that the righteous man might fall seven times, yet rises again; but the wicked stumble when calamity strikes (Proverbs 24:16 AP).

The question is, how soon will you get back up? Don't let yesterday's defeats bind up your today.

9 100? 60? 30? TAKE HEED HOW YOU HEAR

> *"Other seeds fell on good soil and produced grain, some a hundredfold, some sixty, some thirty. He who has ears, let him hear." (Matthew 13:8-9)*

How many times do we receive a word from God and get excited about how He spoke to us? Yet two months later, we look back and it seems like it had little effect on our life. Many things in life desire our attention and desire to take away a work that God has started.

Whenever God speaks, we need to value His word in our life to no end and at all cost.

In Matthew chapter 13 we read,

> *"For this people's heart has grown dull, and with their ears they can barely hear, and their eyes they have closed, lest they should see with their eyes and hear with their ears and understand with their heart and turn, and I would heal them." (v. 15)*

The condition of our heart, what the Bible calls "soil" in Jesus' parable in Matthew 13, determines our ability to hear God's voice and produce fruit for Him. The heart that is set to understand (the "good soil") is what the Lord can use to speak to us; and as a result, we will bear much fruit.

The enemy's goal is to keep us from receiving the Word, whether it's by distracting us, by convincing us we cannot endure, or by telling us we will never understand it.

> *"When anyone hears the word of the kingdom and does not understand it, the evil one comes and snatches away what has been sown in the heart. This is what was sown along the path." (Matthew 13:19)*

In the same way God speaks to us, the enemy of our soul tries to bring negative drama in hopes of distracting us by it. What we hear, whether it is good or bad, takes root in our belief system. When the wrong things begin to take root in our heart, they keep us from hearing God's voice the way we were intended to hear it.

King Solomon wrote, "Above all else, guard your heart, for it is the wellspring of life" (Proverbs 4:23 AP). The heart becomes the filter of the things that come to us in life and also the filter of what flows out of us.

> *"As for what was sown on good soil, this is the one who hears the word and understands it. He indeed bears fruit and yields, in one case a hundredfold, in another sixty, and another thirty." (Matthew 13:23)*

A word spoken has the power to transform a life. Yet two people receive a word, and one's life is dramatically changed, while in the other's life, it seems like nothing ever changes.

We need to have a childlike faith that rises up within whenever we hear God's Word. Only when we take it and believe it, will it change everything in our life. When the heart is pure, it gives us the ability to see God.

> *"But blessed are your eyes, for they see, and your ears, for they hear. For truly, I say to you, many prophets and righteous people longed to see what you see, and did not see it, and to hear what you hear, and did not hear it." (Matthew 13:16-17)*

Let us allow our lives to be transformed whenever God speaks.

> *What we hear,*
> *whether good or bad,*
> *takes root in our belief*
> *system.*

10 BATTLEGROUND IN THE VALLEY

Where is your battleground?

Isn't it the battle that you fight in secret and the cries that come forth when no one knows?

It is in this secret place that God does His most precious work in the lives of His saints. Honor is visible to the public eye, but the deep work of Heaven begins in the lonely place where it's only you and your Father in a dry wilderness.

Our willingness to be okay with God doing a work in the valley determines the direction of our life. We look at those in life who seemingly have an effect wherever they go. What we don't see are the things they had to go through to get to that place.

It would be interesting to know more details of the life of David before he fought the battle with Goliath. What was the whole process that got him there? He was not considered to be one who would be anointed as king, but the Bible says, "For the LORD sees not as man sees: man looks on the outward appearance, but the LORD looks on the heart" (1 Samuel 16:7).

I believe that any person who will ever do anything for Christ and His Kingdom has to be *made* before they have their first major win. If we desire to go on with God to a place of usefulness, there will be a time of wilderness.

If a man has not been through a pit of despair and utter hopelessness and failure, one has to ask if he will be effective in life. The deepest trials we go through are the things that make up who we are in His Kingdom. How can we show someone else the way to deliverance if we ourselves have never been in a pit?

If we are saints, we have no choice but to be tested. To be purified, gold must go through fire. There is simply no way around it. If Jesus Himself was tested, why do we think we would be any different?

How does God test His people? A good example is found in the book of Psalms, chapter 66:

> *For you, oh God, have tested us;*
> *you have tried us as silver is tried. You brought us into the net;*
> *you laid a crushing burden on our backs;*
> *you let men ride over our heads;*
> *we went through fire and through water;*
> *yet you have brought us out to a place of abundance.*
> *(vv. 10-12)*

How easy it is to find ourselves in a place where hope seems to be lost. Again, in Psalms 38, verses 5-10:

> *My wounds stink and fester*
> *because of my foolishness,*
> *I am utterly bowed down and prostrate;*
> *all the day I go about mourning.*
> *For my sides are filled with burning,*
> *and there is no soundness in my flesh.*
> *I am feeble and crushed;*
> *I groan because of the tumult of my heart.*
> *Oh LORD, all my longing is before you;*
> *my sighing is not hidden from you.*
> *My heart throbs; my strength fails me,*
> *and the light of my eyes—it also has gone from me.*

What an encouragement for those who find themselves in a dark valley and needing a touch from Heaven! We are redeemed Christians, but that does not make our need less; I believe we become more and more dependent on Him when we face dark lonely valleys.

Depending on Him when we are faced with difficulty is one of the most beautiful things! It's not about trying to stay on the mountaintop; in the depth of the valleys is where we find Him in a special way.

All He wants is a yes from your heart. That's it. A simple yes from a sincere heart will change your life forever and set you on a rock—the Rock, Christ Jesus. A no will hold you back, but yes will give Him permission to cut the dark wounds out of your heart and forever change your life.

Don't let the attacks of the enemy in the wilderness valleys derail you from a life of divine purpose.

How vital that we understand what is going on around us! Many times I've heard "Don't focus on what the enemy is doing." I believe God needs to open our eyes so we can see what is coming against us. If we can be convinced we have no enemy, then the devil's work is loosed on our life and we stand no chance against him. It's time we recognize our real enemies and call them for what they are.

Jesus' experience in the wilderness for 40 days before His ministry started is where He defeated the enemy and gained the upper hand by total dependence on and submission to His Father.

Our only hope for deliverance is going to be to follow His example.

In the depth of the valleys is where we find Him in a special way.

11 INTERCESSION

What is intercession?

For many of my years as a Christian, the word *intercession* did not make sense and I was far from being interested in interceding for people. The thought of praying for someone bored me to no end, but hearing some dramatic testimonies of people who dared to take the sin of other people, bringing it to God and confessing it for them, made my mind go back to Jesus hanging on the cross.

I see Jesus taking my sin and bearing the shame, the guilt, the condemnation. He confessed before the Father, "Father, forgive them; they don't even know what they are doing!" If the Bible tells us to have the mind of Christ, what will we do with the sins of those we rub shoulders with?

Intercession takes the sin of others and confesses it before the Father. There are many things God cannot do unless He finds someone to stand in the gap and confess the sins committed against Heaven.

Unless we humble ourselves, we find it hard to intercede for others. One of the greater sins we face as a Christian nation is pride. Two men went to the temple to pray; one was a proud religious leader while the other was a despised tax collector. Yet the one who went home with Heaven smiling on his life was not the one who thought he was right, but the one who saw his need for the only One who is right—Christ.

Intercession becomes a real part of our lives only when we see our lack and confess a sin committed against Heaven by ourselves or others in the same way Jesus did.

Understanding the cross is understanding forgiveness. There is no way to receive the blessing without forgiveness. Jesus took the cup of our sin and counted it an honor to suffer. He counted it pure joy and despised the shame.

Will you drink the cup set before you?

12 DISCOVERING THE PEARL

How can a man buy a pearl that he has not discovered?

"When a man discovers a treasure hid in the field" is how one translation writes the parable of the Kingdom. The enemy of our soul is good at keeping man from discovering the treasure hidden in the field—many times through distraction—but once a man discovers it and counts the cost, he will give everything he has for the pearl of great price.

"Again, the kingdom of heaven is like a merchant in search of fine pearls, who, on finding one pearl of great value, went and sold all that he had and bought it." (Matthew 13:45-46)

We can't sell out for something we have not discovered; but once we discover, then we can sell out for it! The first step is not selling out, but step one must be to discover the pearl. We must come to know what we are selling out for; we will never sell out for nothing. Only when we discover what this treasure is will we be courageous enough to give up what we have.

If you meet a great salesperson who has a product to sell, his goal is to convince you to exchange what you have for something he has. There is no reason to buy if you don't see the value in his product. The Kingdom is no different—if you don't see the value of it, you will never sell out for it!

13 ASHAMED OF HIS NAME

Luke 12:8-9 presents a personal challenge for us as professing Christians not to hold back when given an opportunity to confess Christ's name in public. If we are called believers in Him, why is it so hard for Christians to be authentic and real when asked about our faith in Christ?

> *"And I tell you, everyone who acknowledges me before men, the Son of Man also will acknowledge before the angels of God, but the one who denies me before men will be denied before the angels of God." (Luke 12:8-9)*

One of my personal heroes in these modern last days is a man by the name of Tim Tebow. Most everybody admires those who aren't afraid to kneel in public and confess Christ on a football field, but few of us would have the courage to do so ourselves!

Confessing or freely declaring that Christ our Savior is the Son of God will cause Christ to declare before the angels of Heaven that we belong to Him. But if we deny Him in public, He will deny us before the angels of heaven.

Our heart's cry needs to be an authentic gospel without shame and filled with boldness—unless for some reason we want to be denied before the angelic realm, the ones who are here to bring protection to us.

It's not worth denying Him. Confess Him freely!

14 That One Thing

Salvation is confessing my sin and, from a heart of sincerity and surrender, believing in Christ as my savior. But what about going on into a place of deeper, everyday one-on-one, where abiding in Christ takes a person into a lifestyle of oneness with Christ and where the Kingdom of God becomes real and we live for a single purpose in life?

Salvation is the first level of Christianity. Living a Kingdom lifestyle is the next level—a level that few seem to be committed to.

The rich young ruler who came to Jesus had one thing that bound up his heart and held him back from going to a higher place.

The Bible says Jesus loved the rich young ruler. I believe Jesus gave him the secret for the next level of victory, the secret of going to new heights of oneness with Christ, going to a level where he had not yet been. But to gain that, the young man had to give up that one thing that held a firm grasp on his heart.

If I were to ask Christ what the one thing is that keeps me from going to the next level of Kingdom living, what would He say? If He says, "One more thing you need to do," can I do it? Or if He says, "One thing you must give up," can I let it go? Or will I walk away, grieved in my heart?

Our problem is that we can become so narrow-minded that all we see is what we can get for ourselves, and yet the most we can have is what we give to Him. When we give it to Him, He keeps it. When we keep it, we lose it.

Christ knows the thing that is holding you back. Don't resist when He puts His finger on the one thing you must do or give up. He's got your best interest in mind.

Don't miss the opportunity to soar to a higher place.

When we are asked to give up our one thing, it's for our benefit, not our loss.

---

15 THE EYES OF GOD

Many times man finds himself in a place where all he can see is here and now, his focus becomes narrow, and a "mission field" becomes a strange word with zero purpose. Man becomes self-focused, and self-indulgence becomes the driving force of his entire life.

However, the call of God is from an opposite perspective. The message of the entire Bible is about God bringing mankind back to Himself. The enemy of our souls wants us to see life through our own eyes, keeping our focus on our own needs rather than on a desire to bring others into a place where true life-changing transformation takes place.

One of the main faults of the scribes, Pharisees, and religious leaders was that they only cared about personal gain and public appearance. Jesus came as a light to expose darkness, and they did not want their dark side uncovered. They chose the darkness rather than the light the Messiah brought.

The Father's goal is to bring us to a place of choosing, for only when we see through the eyes of God can Heaven's Kingdom realm become real to us and we begin to walk in effectiveness, advancing the Kingdom of God and glorifying the life of Christ in a marvelous way.

16 GUARD THEM FROM EVIL

In the Gospel of John chapter 17, we read that Jesus prayed for His disciples. He prayed, "I am not asking that you remove them from the world, but I ask that you protect them from the evil one" (v. 15).

Jesus did not pray that we would have an easy life free from difficulty; He prayed for our Father's protection from Satan's evil. His prayer in the Garden was for us too, that we would stay pure and free from the pollution of evil. Verse 20: "'I do not ask for these only, but also for those who will believe in me through their word.'"

One of the protections from evil that we need is a shield against offense. One thing that's sure in life is that we will face many opportunities to carry offense. An offense that is not brought under the blood of Christ can so quickly contaminate the heart.

This is a testing ground; we will need to decide whether our heart stays free or gets bound up. I see many wounded soldiers who have been hit with arrows meant to bring evil to their heart so that the life of Christ cannot be manifested. A soldier with a heart that is free will be an effective one who brings change that goes from one generation to the next.

In this testing, may our prayer be the same as the one Jesus prayed, "Guard me from this evil."

17 WILLING TO BE MADE IN THE VALLEY

Are you willing to be made in a lonely valley, a place where you lay all your pride and desire to be applauded by man at the feet of Christ? A place where God's perfect will is your only intention?

Are you willing to be made in a place where you learn to love your enemies and you begin to understand a few of the pains Jesus must have felt when He took your sin and shame on Himself and endured the cross? The natural image of Jesus was so destroyed that He became unrecognizable; He was despised and rejected, forsaken by His best friends, and forsaken by His Father.

In the valley, we can say with Him, "Yea, though I walk through the valley of the shadow of death, I will fear no evil: for thou art with me; thy rod and thy staff they comfort me" (Psalm 23:4 KJV).

Many a life is transformed in the valley, for in the valley we can see our need for a higher power; in the valley we can see the need to humble ourselves and sell everything we have for His Kingdom.

The one who is rich has little material need, and often he finds it difficult to see his own real and deep needs. The help of the Most High is available to all of us, but the question is, do we recognize our own dire need? Or are we trying to make it through life with the strength of our own hand?

Depending on God often will look like the least of seeds; but once established, this seed that is sown becomes the largest and strongest of all plants!

18 THE FEAR OF THE LORD

"The fear of the LORD is the beginning of wisdom," says Proverbs 9:10. So what is the fear of the Lord?

Do you tremble at the thought of His marvelous name? Is there a weight of conviction when His presence surrounds you? When the Holy Spirit shows up, revival cannot be faked; that's why the Bible says the man who trembles at God's word is blessed (Isaiah 66:2). There will be a holy awe when His Spirit shows up.

One of the things we all wish for is revival, but many things that are called revival are entertainment and leave a person carnal with no change, no awe, and no conviction of sin. Not so with the Holy Spirit! When His presence shows up, there is no room for carnality or loose living.

Are you one of those who try to leave when His presence shows up, or are you one of those who run to the place where the Holy Spirit is at work? Wherever conviction falls and the Holy Spirit shows up, our hearts must be before Him in reverence!

In the book of Daniel we find a great example of a man who feared God; Daniel did not bend to the opinions of man when it would have been convenient to do so. He prayed to his God when it was completely forbidden according to public law.

After a fast, Daniel saw a vision, and a key verse tells us why he got an answer to his prayer.

> *And behold, a hand touched me and set me trembling on my hands and knees. And he said to me, "Oh Daniel, man greatly loved, understand the words that I speak to you, and stand upright, for now I have been sent to you." And when he had spoken this word to me, I stood up trembling. Then he said to me, "Fear not, Daniel, for from the first day that you set your heart to understand and humbled yourself before your God, your words have been heard, and I have come because of your words." (Daniel 10:10-12)*

Daniel had the fear of the Lord, and when he set his heart to understand and humbled himself before God, I believe God saw a man who could be trusted. As a result, God used Daniel in a mighty way to show him the future for God's people.

19 THE GLORIFIED CHRIST

> *"But I tell you the truth, it is to your advantage that I go away; for if I do not go away, the Helper will not come to you; but if I go, I will send Him to you." (John 16:7 NASB)*

The only way this written Word is not true for us is if the Holy Spirit is not real to us. Is His presence real? Do we believe in Him in a real and undeniable way? When the Holy Spirit becomes our best friend, this Scripture begins to come together in a real way.

To the carnal man, it would seem much better to have Jesus here in the natural, but the one who walks with the Spirit rejoices that Jesus Christ made a decision to leave and send the Comforter as the One who is here to help guide and direct us in all our ways.

The Scripture that fascinates me is the one where Thomas says, "Unless I put my finger in his side, I will not believe" (see John 20:25).

Jesus did not say in response to Thomas, "If you don't believe, why should I show up for you?" He knew Thomas needed a manifested experience, and because of that, He appeared to His doubting disciple!

If I struggle with doubt, is Christ not able to settle it? I believe He knows the condition of my heart and my desire to know Him. He loves to shatter all my doubts and unbelief; and for this reason, I must not limit Him!

A Christ who appears is wonderful and glorious, but so is the working of the Holy Spirit. The Holy Spirit must be a real experience, a real presence who becomes my best friend, even when my natural man cannot see Him.

As physical beings, we long to see Heaven in physical form. We desire something that the carnal man can connect with—physical matter. Let's not forget that we live in a body, but we are a spirit. A man who believes without seeing in the natural is called a man of faith. Walk by faith and not by sight.

20 REMEMBER LOT'S WIFE

"Remember Lot's wife. Whoever seeks to preserve his life will lose it, but whoever loses his life will keep it." (Luke 17:32)

There are many things in the last part of chapter 17 in Luke for which we might desire more understanding. When will Christ return? What will the Kingdom of God look like? And why should we remember Lot's wife?

Back in the days when Jesus had His feet on this earth in a natural way, natural men tried to understand things according to what they knew of physical matter, and they never "got it." The natural man cannot completely understand all that Jesus is saying here. In order to see things of the spiritual realm, we must go beyond our natural ability and see by the Spirit of God.

One of the main points in this part of Luke 17 is a statement the natural man cannot understand: If we seek to save our life, we will lose it; if we lose our life, we will save it.

What happened to Lot's wife illustrates this truth. She could not let go of the things that were dear to her natural man. There were many things back in Sodom that held her emotions and she had to look back, still tied to that life. As a result, she lost her life as she was turned into a pillar of salt.

Are we holding on to things that we claim as our possessions? Are we holding on to carnal parts of our old life?

Letting go is one of most difficult and yet most rewarding things we will ever learn to do in the Christian life. The moment we start holding on to things, we begin to lose. The moment we let go, we begin to gain. Life is not about controlling but about learning to let go.

When we let go, we surrender to Christ, and then we begin to understand things that we could never understand before. Then He can speak what He wants, and a pure heart is ready to receive and understand.

21 ASK AND KEEP ASKING

And he told them a parable to the effect that they ought always to pray and not lose heart. "And there was a widow in that city who kept coming to him and saying, 'Give me justice against my adversary.'

"And will not God give justice to his elect, who cry to him day and night? Will he delay long over them? I tell you, he will give justice to them speedily. Nevertheless, when the Son of Man comes, will he find faith on earth?" (Luke 18:1, 3, 7-8)

Breakthrough is not for those looking for ease. It takes persistent faith. Many times, the person who knows something has to change is the one who receives a miracle. When our back is to the wall and we have no other option, we find the courage to seek God with whatever it takes.

This was the case of the blind man in Mark chapter 38.

He began to cry out and say, "Jesus, Son of David, have mercy on me!" And many rebuked him, telling him to be silent. But he cried out all the more, "Son of David, have mercy on me!" And Jesus stopped and said, "Call him." And they called the blind man, saying to him, "Take heart. Get up; he is calling you." (Mark 10:47-49)

The blind man could have listened to the ones who were trying to silence him. Who are we listening to? Today we have the Holy Spirit living inside us, and when people try to get us to go with the flow and conform to the standard of this world, Christ's Spirit wants to raise up a standard within us and keep us from being content with a low-level standard.

We'll have many obstacles in this life, and we need the heart of a soldier—a strong soldier with the strength to fight.

Fight the good fight of the faith. Take hold of the eternal life to which you were called and about which you made the good confession in the presence of many witnesses. (1 Timothy 6:12)

We will do well to allow the Spirit to develop in us a persistent faith and confidence in our God.

22 A ROOT OF UNWANTED

Every tree has a root system. It is the root system that feeds the tree. When there is a bad root, it cannot absorb the moisture available to feed the tree. If the root system is corrupt, the tree will always struggle.

The good thing is this: the Bible says the axe is laid to the root of the tree! Whenever a corrupt root system is cut off, it will stop poisoning the tree. The best way to get rid of poison and malnutrition is to separate the bad root from the tree and grow a good root system.

We can pick bad fruit off a bad tree all day long, trying to get rid of the fruit, but it is foolish to think that removing fruit will get rid of a bad root. But once the Holy Spirit reveals to us the root problem, it becomes rather simple to take care of it. Through God's Word and faith, we are given the ability to cut off all negative roots.

How can I know what root is taking energy from my life? This is where the Holy Spirit works; if we come to God and ask Him to show us, He is more than willing to enlighten our understanding. I believe the Holy Spirit longs to show His people things that are holding them back.

The good news is that once the root is recognized and dealt with, the whole fruit issue vanishes and that negative root loses its ability to use unnecessary energy. There is overcoming power for this, and it comes when one asks the Revealer, the Holy Spirit.

There are many marvelous testimonies coming out of the truth of laying the axe to the root of the tree.

One bad root many people struggle with is a root of "unwanted." They battle thoughts of not being wanted, whether these thoughts started with rejection by a mother while a child was still in the womb, or through circumstances in life, or from words spoken to them. If one has a root of "unwanted" in their life, many things come out of that root system. It is astounding to what lengths people will go to be accepted by others; and many times, it all comes from a pattern of thoughts that cause a person to believe "I'm not wanted" or "I'm not as good as..."

Man longs to be accepted, satisfied, and well thought of, but the only true acceptance comes from understanding the gift won for us by Jesus Christ, that we are now sons and daughters of God, and then living in oneness with our Savior.

> *But to all who did receive him, who believed in his name, he gave the right to become children of God. (John 1:12)*

> *"Abide in my love... These things I have spoken to you, that my joy may be in you, and that your joy may be full." (John 15:9, 11)*

23 FINDING HIS STRENGTH AND REST

Has your strength been zapped? As Christians, we find ourselves fighting battles that can be overwhelming at times. Many times after a big win, we are zapped of our natural strength. In the life of a soldier, much training goes into preparation to win the battle against the enemy; and after a big win, he has given everything he has and needs a period of rest in order to gain back his strength for the next battle.

Our true battle is not against flesh and blood, but I believe we can find ourselves caught up in fighting battles that are not the *real* battle, and we come to a place where we are exhausted by the pressures that we come up against. This is when we need to find a place of gaining back our strength for both our inner man and also for our natural man.

What happens after a deep spiritual breakthrough when we have experienced an encounter and life-changing event? One thing we need to be aware of is that such an experience does not guarantee we will not be attacked by the enemy of our soul. We like to think we should be strong and courageous after a big win. But don't be fooled; when our physical strength is drained, this can be an opportunity for the enemy to come and bring discouragement.

In 1 Kings we read the account of Elijah killing all the false prophets of Baal. This great victory was more than a man could ever expect to accomplish in the natural. You would think Elijah would be rejoicing and having the time of his life.

> *But he himself went a day's journey into the wilderness and came and sat down under a broom tree. And he asked that he might die, saying, "It is enough; now, O LORD, take away my life, for I am no better than my fathers." And he lay down and slept under a broom tree. And behold, an angel touched him and said to him, "Arise and eat." And he looked, and behold, there was at his head a cake baked on hot stones and a jar of water. And he ate and drank and lay down again. And the angel of the LORD came again a second time and touched him and said, "Arise and eat, for the journey is too great for you." And he arose and ate and drank, and went in the strength of that food forty days and forty nights to Horeb, the mount of God. (1 Kings 19:4-8)*

This account helps us to be prepared and understand what might come after a big win.

What about David in the book of Psalms? This man fought many battles and always came out on the other side. Somehow, at the end, he always found himself strengthened in who his God was.

The LORD is my strength and my shield;
in him my heart trusts, and I am helped;
my heart exults,
and with my song I give thanks to him.
The LORD is the strength of his people;
he is the saving refuge of his anointed.
(Psalm 28:7-8)

And then we read of the time when the Amalekites had raided and burned David's town and taken captive everyone in it. When David and his men returned, all their wives and children were gone.

And David was greatly distressed, for the people spoke of stoning him, because all the people were bitter in soul, each for his sons and daughters. But David strengthened himself in the LORD his God. (1 Samuel 30:6)

I believe strengthening yourself in the Lord can be done in different ways. There are times when we speak to our soul and we tell our soul to trust in the Lord. There are times when we need time in silence. And then there are times when we bend our knees and listen to some anointed worship music.

As a result of strengthening himself in the Lord, David could then go to the Lord and ask for direction.

And David inquired of the LORD, "Shall I pursue after this band? Shall I overtake them?" He answered him, "Pursue, for you shall surely overtake and shall surely rescue."

And David struck them down from twilight until the evening of the next day, and not a man of them escaped, except four hundred young men, who mounted camels and fled.

David recovered all that the Amalekites had taken, and David rescued his two wives. Nothing was missing, whether small or great, sons or daughters, spoil or anything that had been taken. David brought back all. (1 Samuel 30:8, 17-19)

How we find strength is not what's most important; the important thing is that we find the Master's strength and rest so we can be effective for the battles yet to come. Strength should never be sought so that we can live a life of ease. We seek strength so we can be effective and accomplish the mission He has given us.

Saint of God, don't be discouraged; your strength is coming back! And you will find yourself refreshed in His presence. He is faithful. Don't let your sapped strength lead you into despair. Praise God for the encounter, and *know* that your strength is coming back!

24 WHO IS IN CONTROL?

Many times we don't understand our own motives, but there is One who knows why we do what we do. The Holy Spirit can see if we are in charge of our own life or if He's the one in charge.

In every person there's a desire to control what happens next. When we look at all sins, one common thing we find underneath every last one of them is the desire to control and be in charge of one's own life. The Bible says, "Rebellion is as the sin of witchcraft" (1 Samuel 15:23).

Rebellion and witchcraft both demand to be in charge of my own life and to do as I wish, and it's all about what I get out of it. This is nothing more than the carnal man unable to submit to Christ. Sin springs out of "I need to fight for myself because I don't believe God will."

That verse goes on to say, "and stubbornness is as iniquity and idolatry (KJV)." Are we stubborn when the Lord's word touches sensitive parts of our lives? Do we want to do things *our* way?

The Holy Spirit's goal is to bring us to a place where we can truly say, "My life is Yours!"

We see this clearly when Jesus was led by the Spirit into the wilderness. It was in that place of dryness that He became completely surrendered to the power of the Holy Spirit. As a result, this is where His ministry began.

I believe we cannot have a ministry with a solid foundation unless we go through a time in life when it seems like everything dries up and there we learn to surrender to His perfect will.

We all admire those who are being used by God in a mighty way, but what is the story behind their ministry? Unless a person has been tested by God, how can they be trusted? Every person is born into sin, and there needs to come a time when this is overcome, when not only acts of sin are overcome but the sin nature inside the person is dealt with. I repeat, I don't believe we can trust any person who is in ministry who has not gone through a time when everything in his life dried up and it looked like it was over for him.

If Jesus *the Son* was led into the wilderness to be tested in order to overcome the enemy, how much more do we need a time in our lives when we overcome our enemy? The Bible says Jesus learned obedience by the things he suffered (Hebrews 5:8). Yet as humans we go out of our way to avoid all suffering. As humans, no one desires suffering and testing; but let's not forget this is God's way of dealing with His people.

Avoiding the cup that is set before you in life will only bring disaster and a hardened heart.

The sufferings and the tests we face in life have a way of bringing us to a place where we no longer need to be in charge. The good thing is that God is always working for our good, and He knows not only how much we need to learn but also how much we can bear. What He's doing is creating within us the nature of Jesus himself.

The things we go through in life will either soften us or make us hardened and unchangeable. His goal is to bring us to a place of surrender and brokenness, to bring us to a place where we can say

"Your will be done!" Our perfect example is in the words of Jesus asking His Father to remove the cup of suffering He was facing.

> *And going a little farther he fell on his face and prayed, saying, "My Father, if it be possible, let this cup pass from me; nevertheless, not as I will, but as you will." (Matthew 26:39)*

Avoiding the cup that is set before you in life will only bring disaster and a hardened heart. The Holy Spirit is faithful and knows what we need and when we need it. Again I repeat, His goal is to form Christ in us!

> *And he said to him, "You shall love the Lord your God with all your heart and with all your soul and with all your mind. This is the great and first commandment. And a second is like it: You shall love your neighbor as yourself. On these two commandments depend all the Law and the Prophets." (Matthew 22:37-40)*

Loving God with all our heart, soul, and mind and loving our neighbor as ourselves indicates that the self-man has been dealt with and now Christ is captain of our ship. We no longer have the right to demand and control the relationships in our life. We simply learn to surrender and allow Him to guide and direct our life in the direction He wants us to go.

25 "I FORGIVE"

> *"Pay attention to yourselves! If your brother sins, rebuke him, and if he repents, forgive him, and if he sins against you seven times in the day, and turns to you seven times, saying, 'I repent,' you must forgive him."*
>
> *The apostles said to the Lord, "Increase our faith!" And the Lord said, "If you had faith like a grain of mustard seed, you could say*

to this mulberry tree, 'Be uprooted and planted in the sea,' and it would obey you." (Luke 17:3-6)

We are all a work in progress, just as the disciples were. One of the most important things we must learn as Christ's disciples in this day is to forgive when we have been mistreated. But what about when we are continually ill-treated? It is one thing to be violated once, but what about when the hurt becomes a reoccurring thing?

When Jesus told the disciples they needed to forgive if they were sinned against seven times in one day, their immediate response was, "Increase our faith, Lord!"

Just as it takes faith for healing or for a complicated situation in your occupation or for a financial breakthrough, it also takes faith for us to forgive those who have harmed us. The natural man finds it completely impossible to forgive when wronged, and this is why it takes faith in order to *make the choice* to forgive. Sometimes forgiveness can only come when our faith is increased.

Isn't part of faith a deep-seated trust in who God is? We see this trust between Jesus and His Father. The relationship Jesus had with His heavenly Father gave Him the confidence as He was dying on the cross to say, "Father, forgive them!" If you don't have that confidence in who your heavenly Father is, how can you forgive?

One of the things that torments our enemy, Satan, is to hear a Christian say, "I forgive!" These were the words that came from Jesus just before the greatest victory that was ever accomplished in human history. The enemy hates the words *I forgive*.

I believe our cry needs to be that we will have a heart of forgiveness whenever we find ourselves on the bad end of the deal. There will always be some situation where we have the opportunity to release those who come against us. We also cannot forget we are human and we have all injured others, whether intentionally or unintentionally. Keeping this in mind helps us remember what to do when we end up being the ones who are mistreated.

There are two options: either we are tormented when wronged, or our enemy is tormented when we have a continuous "I forgive" coming out of our hearts. There are times when there is nothing else to say other than simply, "Increase my faith, Lord" and "I forgive."

Create in me a clean heart, O God, and renew a right spirit within me. (Psalm 51:10)

A prayer: Thank you, Lord, for forgiving me for the times I have violated others, and help me see where I am still harming others in ways I'm not aware of.

Lord, I come before You with a heart grateful for Your giving everything You had to forgive me of my sins. I ask that You create within me a heart that always has an "I forgive" coming out. I welcome the fire of Your Spirit to consume the sin nature within me. Whenever I am mistreated, help me to remember what You did for me on the cross. Today I choose to repeat the words that You spoke on the cross, "Forgive them, Lord!"

Create within me a clean heart. Increase my faith. I choose a life of pure, clean forgiveness. I give all my rights to You. Use me where You want to use me.

26 UNTIL YOU SAY, "BLESSED IS HE WHO COMES IN THE NAME OF THE LORD."

"O Jerusalem, Jerusalem, the city that kills the prophets and stones those who are sent to it! How often would I have gathered your children together as a hen gathers her brood under her wings, and you were not willing! See, your house is left to you desolate. For I tell you, you will not see me again, until you say, 'Blessed is he who comes in the name of the Lord.'" (Matthew 23:37-39)

Blessed is he who comes in the name of the LORD! (Psalm 118:26)

Recognizing those who are sent by God is a must if we want the true blessing that comes from Heaven. The religious leaders and Pharisees claimed they were waiting and looking for the Messiah, and yet they could not recognize Him when He came! As a result, they missed His Kingdom and eternal life.

One important thing we must learn is to recognize those who are sent by God and to bless the work of God around us in other people. Whenever we see a salvation, we need to share the joy of those in the angelic realm:

> *"Just so, I tell you, there is joy before the angels of God over one sinner who repents." (Luke 15:10)*

Don't kid yourself, Heaven takes notice whenever a work of God is being done and you take the time to stop and bless that work. It might look like a minor thing, but why do you think even the angelic realm rejoices when they see Heaven's work being done in the life of a saint?

> *"And the King will answer them, 'Truly, I say to you, as you did it to one of the least of these my brothers, you did it to me.'" (Matthew 25:40)*

Whether the work of God is in the least or the greatest, we need to bless it. How many who heard that a child was born in Bethlehem in a manger never recognized who He was? The natural man would never expect that the Christ would come in such a way—God, born in a manger! He came as the least and left as a servant of all, but was raised in the power of the Spirit.

Unless our eyes are opened to the reality of who He is, we will never see it. The natural man looks at all things that are glamorous and profound, but the one who is born of the Spirit can see the work of God does not always come with an external sparkle.

Do we have eyes and ears to see and hear what God is doing around us? Or are we blinded by the hardness of our hearts?

> *"Blessed are the pure in heart, for they shall see God."*
> *(Matthew 5:18)*

It is only through the power of His Spirit within us that we are able to see and hear His work around us. Let's ask Him to enlighten the eyes of our hearts (Ephesians 1:18) so that we do not miss what is in our midst!

27 A SACRIFICE OF THANKSGIVING

When we bring a sacrifice, it is not because we *feel* like bringing a sacrifice. A sacrifice is brought because we are *choosing* to give something to God. God says He will show His salvation to the one who offers thanksgiving as a sacrifice.

> *"The one who offers thanksgiving as his sacrifice glorifies me; to one who orders his way rightly I will show the salvation of God!" (Psalm 50:23)*

Another translation of the same verse explains it like this:

> *"The life that pleases me is a life lived in the gratitude of grace, always choosing to walk with me in what is right. This is the sacrifice I desire from you. If you do this, more of my salvation will unfold for you." (Psalm 50:23 TPT)*

Maturity is choosing to offer thanksgiving when everything else in life would keep us from it. Our goal should be to walk in a place where our feelings don't make the final decision; what really matters is what is written in His Word. To make this choice can sometimes be difficult, but victory belongs to the one who can walk in a life of gratitude.

When Jesus was tempted in the wilderness, I believe all His human feelings could have agreed to what the enemy was offering Him. The enemy tried to play into His feelings, but His response always came back to "It is written..."! The wilderness was a dry place, but this did not keep Him from standing on the Word. I believe after the third temptation, the accuser saw that Jesus was committed and surrendered to the authority of His Father, and the tempter had no chance of victory.

The greatest defense we have against the devil is the same defense Jesus used in the wilderness. If we are totally convinced about the Word of God and we stand on it and resist the devil, he will flee from us!

Our enemy knows whether or not we are convinced of the power of the Word or if we tend to slide into negative thought patterns. God's Word is without flaw, and we have the power to stand on it with a grateful heart.

> *"Man shall not live by bread alone, but by every word that comes from the mouth of God." (Matthew 4:4)*

A true heart of thanksgiving is one of our greatest weapons against any accusing voices. Your greatest victory is as close to you as learning to stand on His Word! There is no more sure foundation than the foundation of His Word.

> *"Heaven and earth will pass away, but my words will not pass away." (Matthew 24:35)*

Let us offer a sacrifice of thanksgiving, for His Word tells us we have been redeemed, saved, and set free. He brought us out of a pit of miry clay and set our feet on a rock. That rock is Christ, and He is the Word of God.

28 THE COMING OF A NEW KINGDOM

Man's natural desire is to control his own life and his own situations; it's a natural thing to do. But not so in Christ's Kingdom. His Kingdom is not a natural kingdom, and it is not of this world. It can only be grasped by the spirit of man through the Spirit of God.

The source that drives your life is what makes the difference between living in the Spirit and living with your eyes fixed on this natural life. Who is in control? What inspiration leads you—your own ideas, or His Spirit? His presence and His thoughts need to be our everyday source of motivation.

The natural man is self-seeking and always looking to steal the glory that belongs to God. The man who loves to give glory back to God is not in control of his own life but is surrendered to the One who has the power to do whatever He desires with our lives.

When we think about the Kingdom of light and the kingdom of darkness, we see clearly that there is a war going on. Satan is trying to steal what rightfully belongs to God. We need to say in our heart, *I never want do anything against God's Kingdom of light.*

If we are feeding the natural man above the spiritual man, we are playing right into the hand of the kingdom of darkness, without even knowing it.

Only the Holy Spirit can open our eyes and help us see His Kingdom of light and surrender to it.

Jesus answered, "Truly, truly, I say to you, unless one is born of water and the Spirit, he cannot enter the kingdom of God. That which is born of the flesh is flesh, and that which is born of the Spirit is spirit. Do not marvel that I said to you, 'You must be born again.' The wind blows where it wishes, and you hear its sound, but you do not know where it comes from or where it goes. So it is with everyone who is born of the Spirit. " (John 3:5-8)

The natural person does not accept the things of the Spirit of God, for they are folly to him, and he is not able to understand them because they are spiritually discerned. (1 Corinthians 2:14)

Whenever we walk with the natural man in charge, we are blinded to seeing the Kingdom of light. Our understanding becomes darkened and a surrendered life looks like foolishness. The natural man asks, *Why should I surrender when I can be in charge of my own life?*

The enemy of our souls wants us to think we can control our own lives and we deserve the praise that comes from man. May the Holy Spirit bring us to a place where we are completely surrendered to Christ and we give glory back to our Creator, where it belongs.

Jesus answered, "My kingdom is not of this world. If my kingdom were of this world, my servants would have been fighting, that I might not be delivered over to the Jews. But my kingdom is not from the world." (John 18:36)

The natural man wants to build his kingdom, but the one who walks in the Spirit understands he is not building a kingdom of his own. We are not building our kingdom, but His. Can you imagine how many issues this would settle if this one simple truth would be clearly understood?

It cannot be "My kingdom come, my will be done." It must be "Your kingdom come, your will be done, on earth as it is in heaven" (Matthew 6:10).

The last great outpouring of His Spirit on this earth, I believe, will be the preparation for Christ's return. We all want to see the return of Christ, but He will not come back for the glory of man; it will be the glory of God that is revealed in that day!

Another perspective that I always ponder is in the book of Matthew:

"For as were the days of Noah, so will be the coming of the Son of Man. For as in those days before the flood they were eating and drinking, marrying and giving in marriage, until the day when Noah entered the ark, and they were unaware until the flood came and swept them all away, so will be the coming of the Son of Man." (Matthew 24:37-39)

In Noah's day, the vast majority of people had completely forgotten who God is and were busy pursuing their own kingdoms.

"Likewise, just as it was in the days of Lot—they were eating and drinking, buying and selling, planting and building, but on the day when Lot went out from Sodom, fire and sulfur rained from heaven and destroyed them all—so will it be on the day when the Son of Man is revealed." (Luke 17:28-30)

So what will the revealing of Christ look like? Many tend to think that we Christians will not pass through tribulation. I do believe that the Lord spared Noah and Lot; however, I believe they went through some rough times. First, it all had to come to a tipping point before they transitioned. I believe what we see in the world today is nothing less than the birth pains of the return of Christ. In order for God to bring in His Kingdom, the kingdom of this world needs to go out. I believe we do not need to repair the kingdom of this world but rather need to pray for the coming of the new kingdom—His Kingdom!

"And I will show wonders in the heavens and in the earth, blood, and fire, and pillars of smoke. The sun shall be turned into darkness, and the moon into blood, before the great and terrible day of the LORD come." (Joel 2:30-31 KJV)

The coming of the Son of Man—it will be great and terrible at the same time. Great for those who love Him and terrible for those who fight against Him. Those who are seeking their own kingdom might be those who say, "Lord, don't come back now." But the one who longs for His appearing says, "Even so, Lord Jesus, come!"

May His Kingdom come, His will be done!

29 UNDERSTANDING REPENTANCE

For many years I felt condemnation whenever a preacher preached on the subject of repentance. I believe we need to understand that repentance is not condemnation! The Bible says that repentance is a gift.

Is it simply the ability to think higher? When I say "think higher," I'm saying "think God's way." Turn from my sin, and see it as He sees it.

When the Holy Spirit brings a word, you turn to that way of thinking and forsake your old thought life. You step up to a higher way of thinking and reject the old thought pattern that led to sin, whether the sin is in acts or in a way of thinking.

Repentance is the ability to see there is a higher way. Sin is a low life, but often we don't see it and we fail to think higher. To repent is to turn back to God and think His way. Sin is me fighting for myself. God says, "Come up higher and think the way I think, and I, the Lord, will fight for you!"

Keep in mind that sin takes our rights—our right to be free, our right to be pure. Sin binds us and puts us in prison. Repentance takes us back to freedom and puts us on a higher road. Repentance is a gift that we put into action and that will bring about a change in the heart.

> *And saying, "The time is fulfilled, and the kingdom of God is at hand; repent and believe in the gospel." (Mark 1:15)*

Repenting and believing the gospel will change the way we think in the deepest places of our hearts. The things we think are true will change when repentance and believing become a part of our lives. God never designed for us to be under condemnation; as a cure, He gives us the gift of repentance and believing the gospel.

The Holy Spirit brings conviction as an invitation to think on a higher level for redemption. The Holy Spirit does not bring conviction for condemnation but for redemption. The enemy of our soul is the one who loves condemnation, and he hates to see God's people free of it!

30 A CRY IN THE WILDERNESS

One can wander about in life, wondering what his calling is and where he is to walk. I believe God knows what path He has for each person and knows how to get them there.

Whenever God puts a calling on a person's life, the first thing the enemy wants to do is stop that calling from coming together or slow it down. This can be done in many different ways, whether with simple distraction or causing wounds and hurts to the point we can't even function in the calling God has for us.

The good thing is we have a friend who was sent to us after the resurrection of Jesus. He knows all things, and to Him, there are few secrets, if any. On our own, we will never fully comprehend the secrets that come from our Father's heart. But we have a friend who speaks to us if we only take the time to hear and silence all distractions. If there are things blocking us from hearing, He knows exactly what they are. He has set many people free and brought them to a place of hearing the Father's voice. It's an easy thing for Him to undo years of emptiness and void.

There is a reason why Jesus said, "It is good for you that I go to my Father" because He knew when our friend the Holy Spirit is released and we depend on Him, deliverance will come!

One calling that fascinates me is that given to John the Baptist. The Bible says he was a voice crying in the wilderness. A wilderness is a place that is not populated; it can be dry and empty. But out of that dry and empty place, there was heard a voice of one crying to "prepare the way of the Lord" (Matthew 3:3).

Perhaps you have thought, *The place where I'm walking feels empty and dry*. John the Baptist was a voice that was needed for the ministry of Jesus' first coming. Is there a voice needed for the second coming of Christ? I believe many who find themselves in a wilderness are a perfect voice to be heard in the last days!

Just because you are in a dry and barren land does not say you can't have a cry for His second coming. Jesus defeated the enemy in the desert. John the Baptist was a voice crying in the wilderness.

The place you are walking today is no accident. What an opportunity to be one who ends up being a voice in a wilderness! Your land might feel like it's God-forsaken, but that is where He meets His people. He came for those who need water, not for those who don't need Him.

Even the person who speaks no words in public sometimes carries a loud voice; it just can't be heard by natural ears. The way you live and the way you treat people sometimes speak at a greater volume than any natural sound that could ever come out of your mouth. I believe people can tell quickly if you are a person who is ready to slice and cut apart, or if there's brokenness and true humility inside.

---

*The place you are
walking today
is no accident.*

If you find yourself in a place where it seems like you're not moving forward, my encouragement is to keep sowing the seed of righteousness, even when it doesn't look like anything is happening.

*He put another parable before them, saying, "The kingdom of heaven is like a grain of mustard seed that a man took and sowed in his field. It is the smallest of all seeds, but when it has grown it is larger than all the garden plants and becomes a tree, so that the birds of the air come and make nests in its branches."
(Matthew 13:31-32)*

"And everyone who has left houses or brothers or sisters or father or mother or children or lands, for my name's sake, will

receive a hundredfold and will inherit eternal life. But many who are first will be last, and the last first." (Matthew 19:29-30)

Sow the right seed; it will eventually grow. It's just a matter of time. It's not for you to say how long it will take for a seed to grow, but it is your job to keep on sowing and watering. Keep doing what is right, and it's only a matter of time until God will reward you for doing the right thing. You might not have arrived yet. Or you might not know with clarity what the Lord's calling is on your life, but keep sowing the seed of righteousness, and it will come to pass.

The hardest part of sowing is that sometimes you simply can't see if anything is happening; however, this is not the time to be discouraged.

> *Be patient, therefore, brothers, until the coming of the Lord. See how the farmer waits for the precious fruit of the earth, being patient about it, until it receives the early and the late rains. You also, be patient. Establish your hearts, for the coming of the Lord is at hand. (James 5:7-8)*

Oh the glorious place that a man can walk when he places his whole life into the hands of his Creator!

> *So is it with the resurrection of the dead. What is sown is perishable; what is raised is imperishable. It is sown in dishonor; it is raised in glory. It is sown in weakness; it is raised in power. It is sown a natural body; it is raised a spiritual body. If there is a natural body, there is also a spiritual body. Thus it is written, "The first man Adam became a living being"; the last Adam became a life-giving spirit. But it is not the spiritual that is first but the natural, and then the spiritual. The first man was from the earth, a man of dust; the second man is from heaven. As was the man of dust, so also are those who are of the dust, and as is the man of heaven, so also are those who are of heaven. Just as we have borne the image of the man of dust, we shall also bear the image of the man of heaven. (1 Corinthians 15:42-49)*

Jesus gave His life as a seed and was raised as the Savior of the world. He was willing to take the cup and drink it; and today, He is the most glorified person who ever lived. But His body was sown as a seed of dishonor and was raised in glory. He became a powerful voice because of what He was willing to pay. The question to us today is: How much are we willing to pay in seed?

We are not paying for our salvation; that is not what this is about, because Jesus Christ already paid for that. But we will receive in this life—and I believe in the next—according to what we are willing to lay down as seeds of righteousness.

31 WITH ALL YOUR GETTING, GET UNDERSTANDING

Heaven knows how much we need an encounter with Christ in a real way. We cannot afford to live life without knowing the One who died for our sins. When our understanding becomes dark and we can't comprehend what life is all about, we fall into a deep pit of despair.

We need a real understanding that what Jesus did for us on the cross is one of the most-needed things in our lives. One of the amazing things about salvation is that our eyes are opened to the reality of who Christ is and what He has done for us. There are many levels of knowing and having a relationship with Christ Jesus; and the more time we spend with Him, the more the Holy Spirit fills us with wisdom and understanding, and the more our lives are transformed.

The Bible says, "In all your getting, get understanding" (Proverbs 4:7 NKJV). The understanding that we need is understanding downloaded from Heaven into our whole being, spirit, soul, and body. "Understanding" is a vital part of moving forward in who we are in Christ and His calling on our life.

Wisdom is the principal thing; therefore get wisdom: and with all thy getting get understanding. (Proverbs 4:7 KJV)

The fear of the LORD is the beginning of wisdom, and knowledge of the Holy One is understanding. (Proverbs 9:10 NIV)

In the lips of him that hath understanding wisdom is found: but a rod is for the back of him that is void of understanding. (Proverbs 10:13 KJV)

How easy it is to forget that wisdom begins with the fear of the Lord and knowledge of the Holy One is understanding. We have access to the nature and mind of God. And it is open to those who will fear God and seek the knowledge of the Holy One, because this will bring understanding.

If knowledge of the Holy One and the fear of the Lord are present in your life, what more do you want?

. . . . .

What are we after in life? What is it that we want? If we are not setting our sights on His Kingdom, we go about in life busy trying to get many things; but the truth is, one thing is needful. The reality is that many times we don't believe that seeking His Kingdom first is truly rewarding.

The Bible does not tell us to seek His Kingdom first for no reason; He has our best interest in mind and He is looking out for us.

Seeking true riches from Heaven causes us to stop and think about how we treat other people. What will we be known for after we exit this world? We can be people with much so-called success, but what truly matters is the effect we have on other people. We can have either a positive effect or a negative effect. Are we known as people of mercy, or do we want justice for everything done against us? When we walk into a room, what presence do people detect? Is it mercy, or is it a harsh judgment? You might have had a difficult life, but that should never be an excuse to be a negative presence. We are called to be a city on a hill, radiating the person of Jesus Christ!

If there was ever a person who understood what it meant to give without restriction, it was Jesus. As He hung on the cross, fighting for His last breath, He became the perfect example of what our life and mindset needs to be. He was led as a sheep to the slaughter, and He opened not His mouth because He understood that He would never be His own defense.

The things I can do to defend myself will never be enough to bring resurrection life to my situation. But once I recognize and understand there is One who goes before me and fights my battles when I have no strength to do so myself, then will I walk in true victory! He has an unlimited supply of power, more than I can ever use, and will never run out. It's called the Holy Spirit.

For three days after Jesus' crucifixion, it looked like all hope was lost and there was nothing that could be done. But what people could not see was the Spirit of God at work, and everything was about to change.

The resurrection of Jesus Christ needs to be real in the heart of every believer. For when we believe in a resurrected Savior, our perspective on life will dramatically change.

The people who walked in darkness have seen a great light; those who dwelt in a land of deep darkness, on them has light shone. (Isaiah 9:2)

Having the eyes of your hearts enlightened, that you may know what is the hope to which he has called you, what are the riches of his glorious inheritance in the saints. (Ephesians 1:18)

32 DON'T WASTE YOUR DESERT

Finding our place in life can be a difficult path and many times the difficulties are what it takes to make the person that God intended for us to be. If life would be nothing but ease, many of us would never decide to give God our everything, forsaking the self life. Jesus had to go through a desert; what makes us think we don't need this same testing ground? I believe Jesus could have resisted the desert because He had free will, but He chose to go through and be an overcomer. This choice would eventually lead to saving many lost souls from eternal damnation.

The desert is meant to dry up everything in our life that is not from above. The desert is meant to test our core values and bring out the things in our life that still need to be changed.

Most likely we would never choose to walk in a dry desert if we had a choice. The Bible says the Spirit led Jesus into the desert to be tempted by the devil.

> *Then Jesus was led up by the Spirit into the wilderness to be tempted by the devil. (Matthew 4:1)*

We would not say the Holy Spirit would lead us into a drought for our good, but many times our actions prove different when we fight the drought, looking for escape from the dry, empty places, resisting anything God wants to do in our lives. I believe when God begins to work in a person's life to bring him to a place to be useful in God's Kingdom, the wilderness is many times where He starts!

If we could only hear the heart of our Father, it might go something like this: "Have you considered my servant Job? Even when you take everything away from him, I believe at the end My name will still be glorified, because he knows everything good comes from Me and he will end up showing the world he is not dependent on a life of ease, but on my Holy Spirit."

Whether it's fire or drought, it's meant to purify our inner man and rid us of any baggage that wants to hang on to our life. Isn't this a reflection of what biblical fasting is all about? We don't allow our natural man to be in charge of our life. If the Holy Spirit could lead Jesus into the desert, does not the Holy Spirit lead us to biblical fasting? It looks like the desert was directly connected to Jesus fasting for 40 days.

Then Jesus was led up by the Spirit into the wilderness to be tempted by the devil. And after fasting forty days and forty nights, he was hungry. (Matthew 4:1-2)

For all who are led by the Spirit of God are sons of God. (Romans 8:14)

When we think of being led by the Spirit of God, do we think about a life of ease? We need to be careful; the Holy Spirit is the author of peace, but this does not guarantee ease. Ease can be destructive if it's not a place where we find rest in who He is. However, He is the one who comforts us when we need rest. Never seek ease. Seek rest, and strength will follow.

Our soul needs to find rest in Him even in the midst of drought. I believe Jesus found that place of total victory when He resisted every temptation that came to Him in the desert.

So today, if you find yourself in a place of desert or wilderness, don't waste it. This is a great opportunity—an opportunity to come through in the power of the Holy Spirit! I believe our Father is expecting us to be purified. A test and a temptation are not meant for you to see the other side or to always see the answer, but for you to learn to trust Him.

What makes a test? When the answer is not always clear! It's a matter of going through and coming out cleaner, purer, and looking more like Christ.

If that's not what happens in a test, then we must conclude that we have failed the test and it will have to be repeated. Allow the test to do what it was designed for, and the name of Christ will be glorified in a tremendous way.

We have a tendency to think, *Next time I go through this, I will know exactly what is happening,* and this can be partially true, but I believe a test will always be something that needs to be endured, not knowing the exact outcome.

Once we learn to endure and resist the temptation to take an easy way out, one could conclude the test has served its purpose.

Don't waste your desert or wilderness.

33 TWO BRILLIANT OLIVES

Go with me for a moment to the story of two brilliant olives. They both ripen on a tree to a bright green color. One day their master comes along and handpicks both of them. One olive makes it to the olive press, and the other gets lost along the way. At first, it seems like the second olive has a much better life than being crushed by the olive press. But it slowly begins to rot.

Both lose their identity and their life. The one who is lost never becomes useful, but the one who is crushed ends up being used in an inspiring way, bringing flavor wherever it goes.

The path of crushing is never easy but it needs to be chosen over the path of ease.

> *For whoever would save his life will lose it, but whoever loses his life for my sake will find it. (Matthew 16:25)*

> *In your struggle against sin you have not yet resisted to the point of shedding your blood. And have you forgotten the exhortation that addresses you as sons? "My son, do not regard lightly the discipline of the Lord, nor be weary when reproved by him. For the Lord disciplines the one he loves, and chastises every son whom he receives." It is for discipline that you have to endure. God is treating you as sons. For what son is there whom his father does not discipline? (Hebrews 12:4-7)*

The first disciples of Jesus understood this, and most of them ended up giving their physical life for the sake of the gospel. They counted it a joy to be persecuted for the name of Jesus.

34 IF GOD WROTE A LETTER

You used to have a flame that was burning bright, A heart that was on fire. An energy that was pure and clean. I'm calling you back, back to the place where your zeal is for Me, and Me only. One touch from My Holy Spirit will renew your strength, and the fire you had will once again be rekindled!

I long to be the lover of your soul. What I want is simply to have time with you, to be your company, where we get to know each other. You think you need passion for Me, but if you could only see how much passion I have for you! All I want is your presence. You think you should long for My presence, but the truth is I already long for you more than you will ever know. My goal was always that My sheep hear My voice. Just as you enjoy the presence of your closest friends, so I enjoy the moments we spend together in your personal prayer time.

My heart burns for the people I created. If only you could hear the thoughts that I think toward you, thoughts to give you hope and a future with an expected end. I never intended for you to be distracted with the carnal things in the natural life. My heart is to have a oneness with you, where you hear the thoughts that come from Me.

Never let the garbage of this world take away My peace in your heart. If you only understood: whenever you get hit with darts from the evil one, all you need to do is stand up and declare the blood of Jesus, and the hurts and wounds will vanish!

There will be times when you get hit so hard that it will be difficult to stay focused on what My work on the cross has accomplished. But don't let this distract you; My blood contains the power to overcome any dart that comes against you. Don't hesitate to call on My name in faith. And I will send forth mighty warriors to your rescue!

Take My Word and hang on to it. Forsake everything in your life that does not agree with who I AM. I will be with you and never forsake you! Even when your feelings say otherwise, My Word stands above everything, including your own thoughts, even when you find yourself in a pit of despair.

Learn to live by My Word, against all circumstances. If you could only understand how solid a foundation is under the words that I left with you, your life would rise to a new level. My Spirit is longing to release power in your life the moment you believe My Word!

The best thing I could come up with to save you from your sins was to send my beloved Son and have Him give His life so that you could go free. Now that He's back with me again, My Spirit has been sent to you, and the only thing that can stop My work is if you don't believe in Him.

35 DID NOT OUR HEARTS BURN?

They said to each other, "Did not our hearts burn within us while he talked to us on the road, while he opened to us the Scriptures?" (Luke 24:32)

This Scripture concerns the disciples right after the resurrection of Jesus Christ. Although it is easy for us to think they should have recognized Him immediately, what about us? If our eyes would be opened to see the many things that take place in our everyday lives, maybe we would be the ones who say, "Did not our hearts burn within us?"

Wasn't it the same situation when the Messiah was born in a manger? To the natural eye, this could not be God, choosing to be born in a lowly manger! But to the ones who had their eyes opened, this was the Christ sent from the Father. If I would have lived in that day, what would I have seen or believed?

It was the wise shepherds who had an angelic visitation and were able to see and follow the star. Even though they could see who He was, there were many who could not see. Shouldn't a king be born in a place of highest honor?

Herod was the king in the day when Jesus was born, but his kingdom was coming to a halt. This was his greatest fear. It's almost a wonder that Herod felt threatened by the birth of Jesus, because of His lowly beginnings. But all wicked kings in Scripture were always afraid of someone taking their kingdom, and they didn't care how many innocent lives were taken as long as their kingdom could be secured.

Herod ordered that all boys two and under would be killed because he felt the life of this baby put his kingdom in peril. Jesus was the exact opposite; He was here to give His life in order to save a lost and dying world. He came to give; everywhere He went He gave everything He had.

We need to be asking the question, "Lord where can I give You more? How can I show You how much I love You?" When our heart burns with compassion and we ask how we can give God more, we are setting up our lives to know Him better.

> And a scribe came up and said to him, "Teacher, I will follow you wherever you go." And Jesus said to him, "Foxes have holes, and birds of the air have nests, but the Son of Man has nowhere to lay his head." Another of the disciples said to him, "Lord, let me first go and bury my father." And Jesus said to him, "Follow me, and leave the dead to bury their own dead." (Matthew 8:18-22)

REVELATION: ONE NUGGET AT A TIME

A commitment to Christ will lead you to a place where you will learn to forsake everything for the name of Christ. A true disciple will learn to leave everything for the sake of the gospel!

Our heart's cry needs to be, "Lord, I want to see the deep things that come from Your heart!"

As we spend time with Him and our hearts cry out for a deeper walk with Him, He will show us who He is.

36 "I WILL, BE CLEAN"

Jesus stretched out his hand and touched him, saying, "I will; be clean." And immediately his leprosy was cleansed. (Matthew 8:3)

The enemy loves to complicate salvation and deliverance, and the church needs to come back to the simplicity of the gospel.

In Matthew chapter 8, the leper needed cleansing, and Jesus made it so simple. All He did was stretch forth His hand and touch the man, saying, "I will; be clean!" Four words and a touch dramatically changed one leper's life forever.

Why do we complicate the gospel? We think the greatest things in life need to be complex, but it is the most uncomplicated that are often the greatest, and many times we miss them because of our highly educated thoughts. We are taught that great things come through education and only those with high IQs can attain these great things. How glorious the simplicity of simply believing in Christ and His ability to touch our everyday situations!

At that time the disciples came to Jesus, saying, "Who is the greatest in the kingdom of heaven?" And calling to him a child, he put him in the midst of them and said, "Truly, I say to you, unless you turn and become like children, you will never enter the kingdom of heaven. Whoever humbles himself like this child is the greatest in the kingdom of heaven." (Matthew 18:1-4)

Many times, ideas we have accumulated in our thought life keep us from true freedom. Unless we turn from our lofty thoughts and receive His Kingdom in the simplicity of receiving without doubt, we cannot enter in. And then Jesus says this way of thinking will make you the greatest in the Kingdom of Heaven. Greatness is not achieved the way the natural man thinks it to be!

In another place, we read that the people in Jesus' day thought they would be heard by God because of their much speaking in prayer. Some prayed on street corners only for public appearance. Greatness is not in many words but in the demonstration of the Holy Spirit and His power. I believe one word spoken by the power of His Spirit can do more than a lifetime of education or intelligent speech. Some of the greatest sermons I've heard have had few words.

This is why the disciples asked Jesus to teach them how to pray. They saw He had a connection with God way beyond what popular education could give. I believe His power came from the time He spent with His Father before the sun came up. He laid His life before His Father in Heaven on a consistent schedule, when no one else was with Him.

Our busy Western culture has a few things to learn when it comes to walking in the power of Christ. We become so busy and so occupied in building our own empires and kingdoms that we give no room to Christ and His power in our lives. We need people who spend more time behind closed doors before the sun comes up.

I don't believe busyness by itself is necessarily bad, but the question is, what are we busy with? If I take my life and sell everything I have for His Kingdom, the Bible says my reward will be great.

Jesus said, "Truly, I say to you, there is no one who has left house or brothers or sisters or mother or father or children or lands, for my sake and for the gospel, who will not receive a hundredfold now in this time, houses and brothers and sisters and mothers and children and lands, with persecutions, and in the age to come eternal life. But many who are first will be last, and the last first." (Mark 10:29-31)

How much have you lost for the Kingdom? If it's done for the Kingdom, you will be rewarded. You may not see it immediately, but never forget it takes a seed a certain amount of time to grow, and the little things you do might take more time than you like, but eventually what you sow will begin to grow.

Let us not complicate the gospel. Jesus never complicated it; He made it simple enough that those who had good soil brought forth much fruit. I believe in these days we live in, our only hope is to go back to the simplicity of the way Jesus connected with his Father and was then able to bring the power He found to those who were ready to receive it.

37 MY KINGDOM IS NOT OF THIS WORLD

Jesus answered, "My kingdom is not of this world. If my kingdom were of this world, my servants would have been fighting, that I might not be delivered over to the Jews. But my kingdom is not from the world." (John 18:36)

If we could understand this one simple truth, it would settle many battles that we were never meant to fight. We get wrapped up in many fights that were never meant to be fought. The natural man sees a natural battle, but Jesus' words tell us our real battles are in a different realm.

We waste much energy fighting battles that don't even matter. We must recognize that the real battle is for His Kingdom to be established here on earth. The only way we will know what battle to fight is through the mind of His Spirit.

I believe many of us respond like Peter did when they came to arrest Jesus; we pull out our sword to fight. His first instinct was to defend the ministry. I don't believe we can point fingers; this was his natural first instinct, and we would do the same.

But Jesus stopped him and said, "You don't understand; I have a cup that I need to drink, and why would I not drink what my Father has assigned to me?"

> *So Jesus said to Peter, "Put your sword into its sheath; shall I not drink the cup that the Father has given me?"*
> *(Matthew 26:52)*

Many of the unnecessary things we go through in life come because we Christians fight our own battles rather than allowing our Father to decide what cup we drink. In the midst of all the pressures we face, we lose sight of this simple truth.

One example is our trying to use politics to fix all the evil that is going on around us. The real battle we're facing is not Republican versus Democrat, but it's good versus evil. The enemy of our soul loves for us to think the battle is between two parties and we somehow need a natural fight. But even though we need to be responsible as Christians, if we focus on the wrong help, we end up using the wrong sword to fight our enemy. When the church becomes effective, we will begin to see things shift without us becoming political about everything.

It was only after Pentecost that Peter was able to give his life for the name of Christ. It was only after being saturated in the power of the Holy Spirit that he became effective and death did not look like it had a sting. He found a new battle to fight, with the Holy Spirit providing the strength and the boldness.

38 OUR GUIDE IN LIFE

We were never meant to be our own guide. The Bible says the Holy Spirit will guide us in the way that we should go. The slightest change in the direction of your life can lead you to a completely different place.

This happened to me one day while I was driving, looking for a place to stop for lunch. I found myself asking the Holy Spirit to guide my path for the day. And I asked Him to guide my every step. It almost made me feel foolish, and I remember asking Him, "Is it impractical to ask You to guide my life in every step?"

When I got on Google Maps, I discovered that I was one road too far north for all the restaurants, at least the ones I was looking for. If I would have consulted Google earlier, I would have turned off one road sooner and then found all the good restaurants with little effort.

This is a huge lesson for us. If only we would learn to ask Him for direction in our life, including our relationships, occupation, church... and the list goes on and on. The Holy Spirit knows everything, and it would be so easy for Him to tell us, "Go this way. Make a right turn, or a left turn." It might take little movement and only a slight turn for your life to head in a completely different direction.

I believe two of the reasons we don't hear the Spirit are that either He is a complete stranger to us, or we are so busy and distracted that we can't hear when He speaks.

One of the first statements of Jesus that we read in the Gospels is when His parents thought He was lost and then they found him in the Temple. He said to them, "Don't you know I must be about my Father's business?" His foundation was well established and He showed great commitment at a young age; He was only here for one reason, and that was to be about His Father's business.

His commitment led Him to be baptized and filled with the Holy Spirit and power. After baptism, He was led by the Spirit into the desert.

Again, in the desert, His commitment had set His heart to go the direction His Father had planned for Him, and then the power of the Holy Spirit guided Him to completely overcome the forces stacked against Him.

The Holy Spirit needs our foundation of commitment in order to guide our lives. Even though He is the one who performs miracles and sets captives free, and it is His power and His power alone that does this, He must have vessels who are completely committed to Him with no reserve!

And though the Lord give you the bread of adversity and the water of affliction, yet your Teacher will not hide himself anymore, but your eyes shall see your Teacher. And your ears shall hear a word behind you, saying, "This is the way, walk in it," when you turn to the right or when you turn to the left. (Isaiah 30:20-21)

Our Teacher will not hide Himself.

39 THE SECRET PLACE

I believe "the secret place" is where Christ's thoughts become our thoughts.

We must have a place where we meet Him, and we need to go there every day. When we have no words to describe where we are in life, when the world seems to be caving in with its stresses and pressures, it's here that we meet Christ and He transforms our thought life. Christ waits for us in the secret place! His hope is that it won't go long until we come back and commune with Him!

I believe on the day we enter through the gates of Glory, we will look on Him and He will not be a stranger to us and we will not be a stranger to Him because of the times we have spent with Him in the secret place. My greatest desire is that I meet Him in secret before I leave this planet behind.

The more we get to know Him, the more confidence we have to meet Him in eternity. We dare not make Him a stranger because if He is a stranger to us, I believe we will be a stranger to Him.

A relationship develops only with much time spent together. If you think about the person in life that you know best, it's only because you spend a lot of time with them. It's no different in our knowing Christ and He knowing us. It's the time we spend seeking the things that are dearest to His heart that will determine how well we know each other.

This is why the Bible warns that we can cast out demons and yet have little relationship with the King. Just because you have power to do His work does not guarantee that you know Him as He intended.

It's quite scary to think how many things we can do in the name of Jesus and yet never know fully who He is. The personal time we spend with Him is more important than what we do in public. (Although our time with Him will determine what effect we have on other—in public.)

I believe Christ has goals and desires just as any person does, and we need to understand what those are in order to fulfill our God-given destiny. Our heart needs to burn for His Kingdom to be established on this earth.

If we could only see clearly how Christ and the Holy Spirit work together to fulfill the purpose of the Father! They are both fully committed to do whatever it takes to bring the Kingdom of God here on earth, and we have the opportunity to join hands and become a part of that glorious Kingdom!

You might have a hard time comprehending things of His Kingdom. But the truth of the matter is that if your heart is set on seeking Him and you ask the Holy Spirit to give you understanding and comprehension, He is faithful and will open up a realm that you have never before walked in. You will look back on your life and say, "He changed my life in such a miraculous way!"

He sees which direction your heart is turned and what your desires are. When you ask Him, He will not deny what you're truly asking for. He wants you to know Him even more than you want to know Him. And He's waiting for your heart to turn and seek Him.

> *"For the eyes of the LORD run to and fro throughout the whole earth, to give strong support to those whose heart is blameless toward him." (2 Chronicles 16:9)*

The Lord is longing to help His people, and all He needs is a heart that is blameless toward Him and looks to Him for deliverance.

The more we look to the Lord for deliverance, the more we value the secret place. Our help does not come from man, but it comes from the One who meets us in secret.

40 THE HOLY SPIRIT AND CHRIST

As vessels, we need to recognize that the only chance we have of walking in His Kingdom is Christ. This is the Holy Spirit's job, to bring us to a place of brokenness and surrender and to develop Christ in us.

There is nothing we can do but give Christ the right of way in every area of our lives. Without this, we have no part in His Kingdom. The more we build a relationship with Christ and welcome the Holy Spirit, the deeper we will go into His Kingdom.

This is our hope, that Christ is formed in us by the power of His Spirit. We need to learn to think as He thinks, so that His perfect will can be fulfilled in our lives.

A life that is filled with pride is always thinking about "my" goals, "my" vision, "my" joy, and "my" pain; but once we give our life to Christ, the only thing that matters is His Kingdom, His power, and His glory. We need to be humble enough to think less often about "me" and more often about Christ.

Holy Spirit, I welcome You to minister to and strengthen Christ in me.

And when we get our focus right, we will also desire to minister to Christ in others.

41 DOES GOD LAUGH AT THE WICKED?

Have you ever wondered why the wicked prosper? On the opposite side, it seems like those who love righteousness can end up trapped in the hand of the wicked. Maybe we can't go by what the situation looks like to the natural mind?

As far as the religious leaders were concerned, they got rid of Jesus the day they crucified Him. It looked like they had accomplished what they were after. To this day, unbelief is still an option. You can believe Jesus never rose from the dead if you want to.

But the man who sees in the realm where God lives sees something completely different. What the religious leaders then couldn't see and unbelievers today cannot see is the Holy Spirit at work!

> *But the meek shall inherit the land and delight themselves in abundant peace. The wicked plots against the righteous and gnashes his teeth at him, but the LORD laughs at the wicked, for he sees that his day is coming. (Psalm 37:11-13)*

The Bible says the meek shall inherit the earth; what it does not say is what time this will happen. We need to move beyond our limited mindset of thinking that if we don't see it now, it must not be truth.

The Lord says a thousand years is like one day to Him. Life is short here on earth, and blessed is the man who can recognize this truth.

The man who is wise says, "I will sow a seed and be patient until it grows. If it takes this seed 120 years to grow, I will be patient and wait and believe for a harvest beyond anything the natural man can imagine."

Have you ever wondered what Jesus' life was like in His twenties? Could He have said at age 28, "This ministry I thought I was sent for is not happening, so I will do my own thing…"? He spent 30 years in preparation for His mission, and it took only 3 years to complete it. Preparation for your calling can take many years, and only Heaven knows what your assignment is and how long it will take to complete it.

God can do more in one day than a man can do in a thousand days. That is why we need to commit everything in our lives to Him, because in a moment, He can release the miraculous in our live

> *There is no limit to*
> *what God can do*
> *when one man commits*
> *everything*
> *into His hands.*

One of the bigger tests that come to us as Christians is mistreatment from those who are closest to us. What will you do with the unrighteous acts of an unbeliever or even a close friend who brings discouragement?

Remember all the ridicule and the mistreatment, persecution, and death that Jesus faced for our redemption. He took every beating on Himself for the salvation of our souls so that we can have a place with Him with the Father in eternity and even now, at this moment.

How could Jesus endure the cross, despising the shame? Hebrews 12:2 tells us it was for the joy that was set before Him. He must have seen His people receiving an inheritance that they never paid for themselves. He was focused on our redemption, not His comfort.

Somehow our eyes need to see what matters in life. When we look at Christ and forget about our own comfort, He is glorified. His name needs to be lifted high, and we need to forget about all our own wants.

Remember how low Christ had to stoop to save and redeem those who were lost in a pit of despair. His heart was torn for those who had no ability to save themselves and were headed straight for a pit of hell. If we could only grasp the depth of compassion that was in His heart to save a dying world, we would forever be changed.

. . . . .

How wicked to think that we can take advantage of those who can't help themselves! One might say it's only wise business to make sure one's company prospers. My question is: Who are you stabbing to get what you want? And who will pay for the wrong done to the orphan and widow?

I believe a healthy dose of the fear of the Lord is the only thing that will change our view on many of these issues. The natural man will always do what it takes to build his own kingdom, regardless of who is brought low through his gain. But Jesus' attitude was the exact opposite; He went low so that we can be redeemed and purchased back.

True humility is only seen in the One who hung on a tree when we ourselves deserved to have been hanging there. He was blameless and faultless. The two thieves on the cross had two different responses to Jesus. One saw this truth and ended up with Christ in Paradise; the other one was still out to get what he wanted to satisfy himself.

Our goal in life needs to be to grasp the things that are dearest to our Lord's heart, the things that are most precious to Him. Only the Holy Spirit can open our eyes to see this.

Christ is coming back for a pure bride, a bride who has been washed from self-interest and self-gain, who has eyes fully focused on Christ, and who knows Him as our redemption.

42 THE GREATNESS OF OUR GOD

> *But do not overlook this one fact, beloved, that with the Lord one day is as a thousand years, and a thousand years as one day. The Lord is not slow to fulfill his promise as some count slowness, but is patient toward you, not wishing that any should perish, but that all should reach repentance. (2 Peter 3:8-9)*

We have our ideas of what time looks like, but God's timetable is beyond our ability to comprehend. In Isaiah we read,

> *"For my thoughts are not your thoughts, neither are your ways my ways, declares the LORD. For as the heavens are higher than the earth, so are my ways higher than your ways and my thoughts than your thoughts." (Isaiah 55:8-9)*

It's astounding that to the Lord a thousand years looks like one day and one day like a thousand years. If we do the math and take a man who lives over a hundred years, in God's eyes, he had two and a half hours. Or, on the other hand, I believe God can take two and a half hours and make it worth a thousand years.

How foolish it must look to our Creator when we think we can take our life into our own hands. We have a God who is able to do more than we can possibly imagine if we would only look to Him for answers. Only wisdom that has begun with "the fear of the Lord" can open our eyes to understand the greatness of our God.

How great is our God? How great is His ability? He has sent His Son to forgive our sins; and not only that, He left His Holy Spirit to minister the deep things from our Father's heart. The Holy Spirit can take the little we give and multiply it a thousand times; or He can do the opposite and take the many things we give and make them as nothing!

> *They said to him, "We have only five loaves here and two fish." And he said, "Bring them here to me." Then he ordered the crowds to sit down on the grass, and taking the loaves and the two fish, he looked up to heaven and said a blessing. Then he broke the loaves and gave them to the disciples, and the disciples gave them to the crowds. And they all ate and were satisfied. And they took up twelve baskets full of the broken pieces left over. (Matthew 14:17-20)*

This was not accomplished with some random power Jesus possessed. Without a doubt, the power of the Holy Spirit was moving. Jesus knew Him. He was not a stranger to the Holy Spirit. He heard from His Father.

You might not have much, but if you give what you have, He can take it and multiply it a thousand times. His power is unlimited, and His mercy is new every morning. It might look like you're giving up everything, but what is offered to Him will be multiplied many times.

43 THE HOLY SPIRIT, OUR HELPER

> *"These things I have spoken to you while I am still with you. But the Helper, the Holy Spirit, whom the Father will send in my name, he will teach you all things and bring to your remembrance all that I have said to you." (John 14:25-26)*

Jesus Christ went back to Heaven and sent the Holy Spirit to be our Helper. How desperately we need friendship with Him and daily communion with our Helper! Recognizing the need for a relationship is our first step to having His help in our life. We need to be reminded of this truth and must begin actively spending time with Him and telling Him He is welcome in our life.

When we have spare time, how do we spend it? We can have many friends in life, but the greatest one we will ever know is the Trinity. Christ forgave our sins, the Holy Spirit is our Helper, and the Source is our Father.

When Moses came down from Mount Sinai, with the two tablets of the testimony in his hand as he came down from the mountain, Moses did not know that the skin of his face shone because he had been talking with God. Aaron and all the people of Israel saw Moses, and behold, the skin of his face shone, and they were afraid to come near him. But Moses called to them, and Aaron and all the leaders of the congregation returned to him, and Moses talked with them. (Exodus 34:29-31)

If you could choose one friend in life, who would it be? Don't forget that choosing the right friend will add many other things to your life. One of the greatest desires a man can have is to talk with his Creator, to commune with the One who made him, the Creator of wind and fire, the One who purifies gold with perfection and holiness.

If we are sincere in this, I believe we will begin to recognize who our Creator is and what His desires are. The closer we get to Him, the more we will recognize who He is.

We love to have Him as our Helper, but we must also recognize there are things that He cannot put up with if we walk close to Him. One of the things that He will bring is conviction where before we had none. Whether it's a word of comfort or a nudge of conviction, both need to be heeded.

Conviction is the ability to see things as God sees them. If we can only see that carrying one little offense committed against us is not worth the short time we have here. The Holy Spirit will bring a true perspective on all offenses, whether small or great. No wonder the Bible says the fear of the Lord is the beginning of wisdom!

When our Helper brings conviction, it's necessary that we thank Him for it and continue to ask Him to show us who He is. A relationship with Him means we listen to Him and hear Him out whenever He convicts us.

. . . . .

The Holy Spirit was the one responsible for bringing Jesus out of the grave. I believe there was a strong relationship between them.

How do you think that the miracles Jesus performed were brought about? Wasn't it by the Holy Spirit? I believe the Holy Spirit was the communication line between Jesus and the Father. If dependence on the Spirit is the way Jesus did His ministry, shouldn't we be doing the same? Or are we better than Jesus and can do it on our own?

We desperately need a generation that comes back to the foundation from which comes all power. If He is our lifeline, our communication line to the Father, why are we not recognizing our dire need for that relationship?

Even the prophets in the Old Testament knew the voice of the Lord would prosper His people. In Deuteronomy, we read that the voice of the Lord will prosper us in many ways:

> "And you shall again obey the voice of the LORD and keep all his commandments that I command you today. The LORD your God will make you abundantly prosperous in all the work of your hand, in the fruit of your womb and in the fruit of your cattle and in the fruit of your ground. For the LORD will again take delight in prospering you, as he took delight in your fathers, when you obey the voice of the LORD your God, to keep his commandments and his statues that are written in this Book of the Law, when you turn to the LORD your God with all your heart and with all your soul." (Deuteronomy 30:8-10)

When the Holy Spirit opens our eyes to see that He is our helper, our life goes to the next level. He is able to give us understanding and comprehension in the knowledge of God. He was the power that created the entire universe by the Word of God, and He has the power to give revelation light.

Let us not forget that true life here on earth begins with receiving Christ and desiring a relationship with Him. Without Him, we receive no forgiveness of our sins. We cannot neglect Jesus Christ, and neither can we neglect the Holy Spirit. God the Father, Jesus the Son, and the Holy Spirit work closely together. One does not move without the unity of the others, and we have the privilege of being a part of the work of the Trinity.

44 THY WILL BE DONE

Jesus gave Himself fully to His Father to the point of death, and the Holy Spirit was there to raise Him up. Jesus was here to give His life completely for mankind, and He never chose honor but chose a place of total surrender throughout His entire life. If you are tempted to think you need to see more return on your seed, think about Jesus and how He chose to live. He chose a low path, completely giving His life with not a place to lay His head and then dying a horrible death.

The Bible says we are to have the mind of Christ. If we take this seriously and live with Him as our model, shouldn't we be okay with our enemies speaking badly of us, as long as we know we're sowing the right seed? It takes a seed time to grow, and who are we to determine how quickly a seed will grow?

I believe if we think this way, we will have a return even in this life, and lack of instant return should never bring despair. Our Father can send rain on the seed that was sown.

> *Be patient, therefore, brothers, until the coming of the Lord. See how the farmer waits for the precious fruit of the earth, being patient about it, until it receives the early and late rains. (James 5:7)*

This verse has been a life verse for me. The Lord brought this to my attention in a time when I was being tested. I believe we keep sowing seeds regardless of whether or not you see an immediate harvest. To stay faithful and keep sowing glorifies our Father in Heaven.

Jesus' willingness to bend low—when it looked to the natural man like a wrong move—is a great example for us. He came to serve and refused to be a king of popularity when the people were planning on taking Him by force and making Him a king.

> *Perceiving then that they were about to come and take him by force to make him king, Jesus withdrew again to the mountain by himself. (John 6:15)*

He left for the mountain for a relationship with his Father rather than a political position. When His Kingdom is established on this earth, it will not be a political agenda and personal power structure. The name of Christ will be lifted high and the Holy Spirit will be there to perform the will of our Father.

45 DOES GOD SEE?

One of the things that the fear of the Lord brings in a person's life is the realization that everything is open to the eyes of God. The smallest offense is not hidden, but rather, it is exposed and open for all to see. We can try to convince ourselves that little offenses don't matter, but the Scriptures say that whatever is not of faith is sin.

When God begins to deal with us, we soon understand that nothing is hidden. The tiniest flaw in us is open and naked before our Creator. Nothing is secret from Him who sees everything.

To the person who has been cleansed and set free, this cleansing and freedom is a glorious reality; but the one who is walking in darkness despises this thought. Light shines in darkness and exposes all the motives of man; this is why the person who has been made right loves the light, but the one who wants to hide his motives can't stand it.

The fool says, "I can hide my sin and nobody will know." On the other hand, the righteous person has learned that "All things are open before my Creator."

> *And no creature is hidden from his sight, but all are naked and exposed to the eyes of him to whom we must give an account. (Hebrews 4:13)*

Another translation puts it this way:

> *There is not one person who can hide their thoughts from God, for nothing that we do remains a secret, and nothing created is concealed, but everything is exposed and defenseless before his eyes, to whom we must render an account (Hebrews 4:13 TPT)*

One fascinating aspect of the character of Jesus was that there was zero hypocrisy; He spoke the truth in love in a flawless manner, and those who could not handle truth wanted Him crucified because it exposed their own evil intentions.

One testimony I've heard from a man who died and went to Heaven said that there were no shadows in Heaven, not even a trace of darkness; everything was light. I believe this indicates there is no hypocrisy there. No darkness. Everything is light.

Why do you think the Bible says that every hair on your head is numbered by God? Doesn't this indicate that He sees every little detail in our lives? Our Creator sees everything in our spirit, everything in our soul, and everything in our body! This should bring much encouragement to the one who is wondering if God sees.

If you have found God to be a merciful God and have given everything to Him, finding that place of brokenness and surrender, confessing all your sins, then you can rejoice in the fact that every detail in your life is an open book!

The eyes of the LORD are in every place, keeping watch on the evil and the good. (Proverbs 15:3)

This is good news for the one who has been washed by the blood and whose conscience has been cleared. This is good news for those who are being aborted before they even have a choice to decide anything in life. A day is coming when justice will be served. We have a God who is just and perfect and all unrighteousness will be exposed.

46 THE WORLD SYSTEM

"If the world hates you, know that it has hated me before it hated you. If you were of the world, the world would love you as its own; but because you are not of the world, but I chose you out of the world, therefore the world hates you. Remember the word that I said to you: 'A servant is not greater than his master.' If they persecuted me, they will also persecute you. If they kept my word, they will also keep yours." (John 15:18-20)

"I have said all these things to you to keep you from falling away. They will put you out of the synagogues. Indeed, the hour is coming when whoever kills you will think he is offering service to God. And they will do these things because they have not known the Father, nor me. But I have said these things to you, that when their hour comes you may remember that I have told them to you." (John 16:1-4)

We look at these Scriptures and we think, *Are these true today?* This has never changed: the world system hates the revelation of Jesus Christ!

The things we value the most determine what system we are under. The world is after self-gratification and all that glorifies the natural man. Jesus had a different value system. He was here to be about His Father's business, not His own. Think about the things that Jesus valued when He walked here, and then think about what the scribes and Pharisees valued most.

As long as we value the glory of man here on earth, the world will not hate us. But once we set our hearts for the glory of God, everything changes. The glory of man is a subtle trap that many fall into. But once the Holy Spirit opens our eyes to the truth and we set our hearts for the glory of God and His Kingdom's values, everything changes. The emptiness of man's glory and the world's values becomes obvious.

The goal of the world system is to disturb the soul and bring chaos to the heart of man. Our enemy does not care how he does this as long as he accomplishes his mission. The sad part is, he can even use those in the church to disturb the lives of individuals. This is why Jesus warned that there will be those who want to kill you, thinking they are doing God's service.

There is only one way to fill the void in man's heart, and that is through the presence of his Creator. We need to set our hearts on the value system of Heaven. If we don't, we will end up being trapped in seeking many things, trying to fill an empty spot in our heart that was never meant to be filled with honor that comes from a system made by man. We become people who are so hungry for the praise of man.

Every individual must check his own values and ask the question, What am I most concerned about? We are all made of the same material, and our Creator understands this. His mercy is new every morning, and He knows how to take us where we need to go. We must set our sail on His value system and allow Him to minister to our soul's deepest needs.

He restores my soul. He leads me in paths of righteousness for his name's sake. (Psalm 23:3)

"Peace I leave with you; my peace I give to you. Not as the world gives do I give to you. Let not your hearts be troubled, neither let them be afraid." (John 14:27)

Our Creator did not design us to walk around with emptiness on the inside. We were designed to be full of life, full and vibrant, not empty and without form, but filled with His presence. The

> *There is only one way to fill the void in man's heart, and that is through the presence of his Creator.*

more we hear His voice and walk with Him in our everyday life, the more healing He brings to the inner parts that only He can heal. His healing has the power to wash away every unhealthy emotion and heal every wound on the inside, whether it came from early childhood or later on in life. This can be a process, but He knows how to get us there!

When we recognize that the world and its values have nothing to offer but more emptiness, our attention turns back to our heavenly Father, from whom all blessings flow. Blessings to the spirit, to the soul, to the body. He was the One who created us in the first place; why could He not also fill every empty area of our lives?

47 THE LEAST OF ALL SEEDS

> *Another parable put he forth unto them, saying, The kingdom of heaven is like to a grain of mustard seed, which a man took, and sowed in his field: Which indeed is the least of all seeds: but when it is grown, it is the greatest among herbs, and becometh a tree, so that the birds of the air come and lodge in the branches thereof. (Matthew 13:31-32 KJV)*

To the natural eye, the Kingdom of Heaven looks like the least of all seeds when it begins. I believe this is why the natural man has a hard time choosing the Kingdom. Most often it looks like the path with least reward. But we must focus our eyes on what cannot be seen, because this seed ends up being the greatest of all plants in the garden. The

King James Bible says it becomes a tree; another translation says it ends up being the largest of all the garden plants.

While Jesus walked on this earth, we see over and over that He took the road of least reward. He was born in a manger. After baptism, He went straight for the wilderness. He endured much persecution, and left for the mountains when the people wanted to make Him king. Washed His disciples' feet. Was a servant to everyone around Him. Ended up being crucified on a cross, where it looked like His Father left Him, because all our sins were hanging on Him!

But the natural man receiveth not the things of the Spirit of God: for they are foolishness unto him: neither can he know them, because they are spiritually discerned. (1 Corinthians 2:14 KJV)

Today, when you have a choice, don't choose based on instant reward. Sowing a seed will take wise choosing. You can't go by what the seed looks like as to whether or not it's the right choice. The Word of God is like the label on a seed packet. Study it, ask the Spirit for understanding, and make sure you understand the great ability of His seed. It will change your life.

48 FROM PRESSURE TO POWER

Child of God, don't you know it is God's favor on your life that allows you to go through pressures? Once we learn to accept the fact that God allows pressure in order to bring power, we are one step closer to walking in a place of victory like never before.

In our natural way of thinking, it would be best to escape trials and pressures that look unnecessary. Praise God that you don't have the smartness to avoid pressure!

It may look like you're way behind where you need to be in life, but maybe God is making a pearl? Maybe He knows what kind of vessel

He is creating? Who are we to look to our Master and say, "Why have you made me this way?" The best you can do is raise your hands high and surrender to the One who will have His way, regardless.

How is it that we think we have the power to make our life what we want it to be? How is it that we so easily forget that somebody else is making our life the way He wants it for a specific reason? Why do we think we need to understand exactly what is being done? The day will come when it becomes clear and without question; once gold is purified, it will be obvious what the purpose was.

Don't forget, surrender and forgiveness are the keys for you to walk in a place that you would never think possible. If you need to raise your hands and forgive, don't hesitate. This perspective will change your life forever.

If you have an option as to when you receive your reward, will you take it immediately and waste it like the prodigal son, or will you go for a long-term investment? The prodigal son knew it was his inheritance and his father did not stop him, but he only had the short-term in mind. Long-term investment is a choice of wisdom. Getting a return immediately is not always bad, but don't forget, long-term is much more important.

The life you live on this earth at most is 120 years, and eternity is forever. I would rather be a forgotten man on earth than a forgotten man in eternity. Sow a righteous seed and leave it to grow. Trust your Father; He will take care of it. Remember Jesus. He chose an eternal reward; He gave His life blood and lost everything He had here but gained a seat at the right hand of His Father. This is why we need to focus our eyes on the things that cannot be seen.

Jesus Christ became the savior of the world, but this did not come through comfort and making choices that felt good to the natural man. He poured out everything He had; it looked like He had lost. But on the third day, the Holy Spirit had something different to say. He brought Jesus Christ out of the grave and forever changed human history.

The revelation we need in our life is the revelation of how Jesus completely surrendered in total dependence on the Holy Spirit. And on God's timetable. Whether we go through a season of waiting or severe testing, let's not forget it's all about giving our life, not preserving it.

49 DON'T PUT CHRIST IN A BOX

In the last couple chapters of John's Gospel, we read that Jesus appeared to His disciples after He arose from the grave. One of the things that I love about these chapters is that John mentions several times that Jesus did many other things that are not written in the book.

Now Jesus did many other signs in the presence of his disciples, which are not written in this book; but these are written so that you may believe that Jesus is the Christ, the Son of God, and that by believing you may have life in his name. (John 20:30-31)

Now there are also many other things that Jesus did. Were every one of them to be written, I suppose that the world itself could not contain the books that would be written. (John 21:25)

We tend to read the Scripture thinking whatever was written was everything Jesus did, but it is obvious that His ministry was much more than what was written in the Bible. We tend to come up with our own ideas about Jesus' life, and we end up putting our Savior in a box where He can't be fully released.

Heaven knows how many times throughout history Christ appeared to His people and performed the miraculous. Even though we have the Holy Spirit with us, why do we limit Christ by saying He would not do in our lives what He did with the disciples? Who said that the appearing of Jesus to His people was over? In Muslim nations, many Muslim people are being converted today through Jesus appearing to them, whether in a dream or an open vision.

Through our religious eyes, we tend to put Christ in a box and limit what He wants to accomplish in our lives. In words He Himself spoke:

> *And he said to them, "You have a fine way of rejecting the commandment of God in order to establish your tradition! For Moses said, 'Honor your father and your mother'; and, 'Whoever reviles father or mother must surely die.' But you say, 'If a man tells his father or his mother, "Whatever you would have gained from me is Corban'"' (that is, given to God)—then you no longer permit him to do anything for his father or mother, thus making void the word of God by your tradition that you have handed down. And many such things you do." (Mark 7:9-13)*

"You have a fine way of rejecting the commandments of God in order to establish your tradition." What a tragedy! Thus the Word of God is made void by our tradition. And then Jesus says, "Many such things you do!'" What a warning for us! How much of this is happening in our culture?

We have many good traditions and practices that we value dearly, but we need to be aware of how these things could keep Christ from doing what He wants to do in our life. How can we balance our traditions and values so that Christ is glorified and we're not operating on a man-made system?

Our foundation must be that Christ is glorified; anything less than this will take Christ out of our everyday life. He must be established in our lives and given the freedom to do what He desires. This is why there was so much conflict between Jesus and the scribes and Pharisees. Those religious leaders polished the outside of the cup and rejected Jesus because of their hidden agendas and religious ideas of who the Messiah should be.

In one place, Jesus even goes so far as to call them whitewashed tombs; inside, they were full of dead bones and all uncleanness, greed, and self-indulgence, destroying the work of God. These were the people who crucified Jesus.

If we want the real gospel, we must be open for correction of areas where we value things above Christ. We should never be people who bring condemnation to those who are not living Christ-centered lives, but there needs to be conviction so that the fear of God can have an effect on a person who is not living for Him.

It's time to release the person of Jesus to rise above all the ideas we have accumulated in our minds. I believe this is why the Bible says in Isaiah there is coming a time when a little child shall lead them.

> *The wolf shall dwell with the lamb, and the leopard shall lie down with the young goat, and the calf and the lion and the fattened calf together; and a little child shall lead them. (Isaiah 11:6)*

> *For consider your calling, brothers: not many of you were wise according to worldly standards, not many were powerful, not many were of noble birth. But God chose what is foolish in the world to shame the wise; God chose what is weak in the world to shame the strong. (1 Corinthians 1:26-27)*

> *So that no human being might boast in the presence of God. And because of him you are in Christ Jesus, who became to us wisdom from God, righteousness and sanctification and redemption, so that, as it is written, "Let the one who boasts, boast in the Lord." (1 Corinthians 1:29-31)*

Why will a child lead them? Isn't it simply because a child has no agenda? Her only goal is love; social status has no hold on her. Humility is the natural personality of a child; she hides nothing. It seems almost impossible for a child to hide her fears. If we could only learn these traits as an adult, we could go so much farther in our walk with Christ!

The biggest problem in our adult relationship with Christ is that we have all these restrictions stacked up that result in putting Christ in a box and restricting the work He came to accomplish. I believe that at the return of Christ there's going to be a major shift in the bride of Christ. Innocence will be restored, just as it was in the garden before sin entered the heart of man.

It will not be for those who are filled with social agendas and pride. It will be for a pure bride, a bride who has only one goal, and that is to allow Christ to be who He is. The moment we put Christ in a box, we are putting ourselves in a box, not Him!

He will return for a pure bride, and we can either join Him or miss Him.

50 HE ENDURED THE CROSS, DESPISING THE SHAME

Looking to Jesus, the founder and perfecter of our faith, who for the joy that was set before him endured the cross, despising the shame, and is seated at the right hand of the throne of God. (Hebrews 12:2)

What shame was Jesus despising? Wasn't it our shame? One of the most crippling things the enemy brings into the life of a person is shame. Fruits that come from shame are hating who you are as a person, craving approval from man, and becoming a breeding ground for the fear of men.

How can we fulfill our God-given calling if we don't like who we are and if who we were created to be can be hidden behind a veil of shame? How can we then fulfill our calling and reach the destination that He has planned for us? Shame attacks the core of who we are and hides our true identity from ourselves and from others.

Many times, it is shame that keeps us from abiding with Him in a place of complete confidence and rest. When shame controls our life, all the purity and innocence that we were meant to walk in is at stake.

We see this in the Garden. Before sin came in, there was zero shame. Adam and Eve were free, with no reason to think differently. However, after sin it was a different story. Sin came and destroyed the confidence they had with God; shame moved in, and death began its vicious cycle.

I believe there's a reason why the Bible says Jesus despised the shame. This is an important part of what He accomplished on the cross. If only we could see that all our sin and shame was dealt with at the cross!

Think about your most shameful moment in life, and then take every disgraceful and guilty moment of every person and add it all together—this and much more than we can imagine was laid on the shoulders of Jesus Christ as He gave His life to redeem mankind from the dark pit of sin and shame.

I don't believe our natural man can grasp how much Jesus suffered for mankind. The physical pain was one thing, but what about all the emotional and mental suffering that He took on his shoulders? All the mental torment that people have faced—and face to this day—has been paid for. This must be one of the things that breaks His heart—the pain that people go through, not having a clue that they could be walking in freedom.

We are called to walk in the mind of Christ, and in this powerful place there is freedom from torment, freedom from physical sickness, and freedom from all sin. This is the freedom that He died for! This opens up a place of confidence, purity, and innocence. Shame has no hold on us!

51 WHEN DO YOU WANT YOUR REWARD?

It's so easy for us as Christians to think, "I sow a seed, and then I will reap." And rightly so. But if we look at the life of Jesus, He chose to receive most of His reward after His time on earth. Most of the time, we want to sow a seed and see instant results; but the most effective sowing may have a harvest after our time on earth. Even though I believe we will reap many things here, we need to keep our eyes on the things that are not seen.

The problem with instant reward is that many times we will settle for the carnal things in life rather than what comes after this life. I believe our greatest reward will come from things that were totally unnoticed or unappreciated.

Jesus went for a prize that cost Him His earthly life. His life was like an olive that goes through the olive press; everything in Him was squeezed out and given for the salvation of man. He had no desire for the glory that came from an earthly kingdom because He knew where His heavenly Father was seated. He had a relationship with His Father that was real and He ignored anything outside of it. If we lose sight of eternal reward, we will sell out for something temporal and empty.

The fear of the Lord is the beginning of wisdom, and one thing that the fear of the Lord brings is the recognition that life is short and eternity is forever.

How empty everything else in life is outside of our relationship with the Father!

52 HAVE YOU LEARNED TO WAIT ON THE LORD?

Do you see a man who is hasty in his words? There is more hope for a fool than for him. (Proverbs 29:20)

How easy for us to respond hastily when we find ourselves on the wrong end of the deal! And how easy it is to think we will sink into a pit of injustice! Children of God, we must understand it is better when Heaven fights for us than when we fight for ourselves. We can be our own defense, but that might be all we will have.

This is the testing ground to prepare us for an eternal destination. If it takes a hundred years for justice to be brought forth, are we good with that? This was one thing that was clear to Jesus. He knew He was not His own defense system, and even though persecution led to death, the Holy Spirit was there to bring Him back.

The question is: Will we trust Him to take us where we need to go? Our life is dependent on faith in our Creator and trusting Him with the entirety of our life. Trust brings faith to life. Our Father knows once we have made a decision to trust Him completely with our life and its outcome.

If you found yourself in the place that Jesus found himself, before the kings of His day, put on trial, accused of things He never did, facing crucifixion, what would be your response?

He was oppressed, and he was afflicted, yet he opened not his mouth; like a lamb that is led to the slaughter, and like a sheep that before its shearers is silent, so he opened not his mouth. By oppression and judgment he was taken away; and as for his generation, who considered that he was cut off out of the land of the living, stricken for the transgression of my people? And they made his grave with the wicked and with a rich man in his death, although he had done no violence, and there was no deceit in his mouth. Yet it was the will of the LORD to crush him; he has put him to grief; when his soul makes an offering for guilt, he shall see his offspring; he shall prolong his days; the will of the LORD shall prosper in his hand. (Isaiah 53:7-10)

There are arguments and belief systems out there that say we must repetitively speak the Word of the Lord in order for it to come to pass. I believe speaking the Word does have power; however His Presence does not always come in words; some of the most powerful words were those that were felt and not spoken. Jesus defeated His enemy with few words. He had set His heart with His Father, and His Presence made the devil nervous.

The first thing we want to do as humans when we are mistreated is to make sure everybody knows that we were not in the wrong. Jesus knew this was not the answer, and He was the most brilliant in knowing how to overcome the enemy. It had to be the Holy Spirit in Him that gave Him the wisdom to overcome and totally defeat all the works of darkness.

> *He gives power to the faint, and to him who has no might he increases strength. Even youths shall faint and be weary, and young men shall fall exhausted; but they who wait for the LORD shall renew their strength; they shall mount up with wings like eagles; they shall run and not be weary; they shall walk and not faint. (Isaiah 40:29-31)*

Waiting on the Lord can be a difficult thing. There is a time to speak, and there's a time to shut up, and it's only by the wisdom of the Holy Spirit that we can walk away without opening our mouth. I believe the more we speak when we find ourselves defending our own agenda, the longer the process of God refining us will take.

One verse that is special to me was brought to me in the midst of a dark time in my life. I woke up one morning with a jolt, and all I heard was James 5:7: "This is God's will for your life." Not knowing what this was, I went to the Scripture, wondering what I would find.

> *Be patient, therefore, brothers, until the coming of the Lord. See how the farmer waits for the precious fruit of the earth, being patient about it, until it receives the early and the late rains. (James 5:7)*

Waiting on the Lord and trusting Him with your entire life is a powerful way you can love Him. To recognize you are not fighting your own battles is to step into a place that guarantees the Holy Spirit will fight for you. We may lose sight of this from time to time, but He has a way of bringing us back and getting us to recognize that He loves to fight our battles.

When we sow seeds of righteousness, we can be confident we will reap if we faint not. Keep sowing seeds of righteousness. Keep watering. You will have a harvest. It's only a matter of time

---

Waiting on the Lord
and trusting Him
with your entire life
is a powerful way
you can love Him.

---

53 A PERFECT REFLECTION

Philip said to him, "Lord, show us the Father, and it is enough for us." Jesus said to him, "Have I been with you so long, and you still do not know me, Philip? Whoever has seen me has seen the Father. How can you say, 'Show us the father'?"
(John 14:8-9)

You can hear the disappointment in Jesus' words in this text. "Have I been with you so long and you still don't know me, Philip?" As Christians, we have been called to represent our Father, to be a reflection of who He is. Could Christ ask you or me, "Have you been a Christian for so long and you still can't represent who I am?"

Shouldn't our personality reflect the Kingdom we live under? We all have flaws and make blunders and have times when we respond out of our carnal nature. But our end goal should be to represent well who He is! Who do we yield to most often—the carnal man, or the man who has been born again?

This must have been what disappointed the devil the most with the early apostles. He could stomp them down and bring them close to physical death; and yet, once they recovered, the fire of Christ came right back and rose up in them like never before. They saw physical torture as only a testing ground.

Count it all joy, my brothers, when you meet trials of various kinds, for you know that the testing of your faith produces steadfastness. And let steadfastness have its full effect, that you may be perfect and complete, lacking in nothing. (James 1:2-4)

The things that come against us should never determine how much of Christ can be seen in our lives. James wrote to count it all joy when you meet trials of various kinds. I believe those disciples understood something that we in our day have a hard time with. I am quick to admit that I love when everything goes smooth and well. But we can't lose sight of the fact that light is most effective in the midst of darkness.

We have been called to be a city on a hill that radiates light. As we approach a time of extreme darkness, when it seems like there is little true light, we need to trim our lamps and need oil that only comes from above.

You might find yourself at the bottom of a pit where nothing makes sense and you can't even figure out why you are there. I know what that darkness feels like, and I know some of the pain that comes with that thought life. But I also know there is a way out! Don't let the darkness of the pit take the cry to be free from your heart. He has delivered many souls out of the pit and the darkness, and He will do it again.

What joy to see a soul who has been transformed from darkness to light being able to reflect the Father of light! We don't always do it perfectly, but the part of Him that we understand and put into action ends up being a perfect reflection.

54 THE CRY THAT GETS AN ANSWER

And the Pharisees and their scribes grumbled at his disciples, saying, "Why do you eat and drink with tax collectors and sinners?" And Jesus answered them, "Those who are well have no need of a physician, but those who are sick. I have not come to call the righteous but sinners to repentance." (Luke 5:30-32)

"Blessed are those who mourn, for they shall be comforted." (Matthew 5:4)

Jesus spent time with tax collectors and sinners because they saw their need. The scribes and Pharisees did not. The tragedy was that the scribes and Pharisees had no idea they were empty on the inside. They had everything polished on the outside, and yet Jesus called them whitewashed tombs.

I believe the desire of Jesus was to wake them up and help them see what their true need was. Yet they refused to hear and became extremely offended when He pointed out their true condition.

Many times we pray about a problem, but think we can "make it" even if we don't receive an answer from God. We have learned to cope with our problems because we think we have so many alternative answers. Once we run out of solutions and see that God is our only source, many times this is when we get answers to our prayers.

Shouldn't we ask Him to open our eyes and help us see how desperately we need our Father as our provider? Maybe we need to refuse to be comforted by false comforts that provide short-term answers? It's almost as though the enemy wants us to be okay with "just enough." This includes all areas of our lives, nothing excluded. The Christian should not settle for anything short of total provision.

When Jesus died on the cross, He paid for all our needs. Nothing lacking. But many times we are okay with half answers, and we can continue without full provision. Isn't this sometimes the thing that stops the miracle power of God in our lives?

In this we can see why a Spirit-led fast is so powerful. We refuse to say, "I am okay. I can make it like this." We refuse all the comfort that our physical body desires, and we choose to see that we need help from a higher power.

> *"And it shall be a statute to you forever that in the seventh month, on the tenth day of the month, you shall afflict yourselves and shall do no work, either the native or the stranger who sojourns among you." (Leviticus 16:29)*

> *But I, when they were sick—I wore sackcloth; I afflicted myself with fasting; I prayed with head bowed on my chest.*
> *(Psalm 35:13)*

Many times we have learned to be "okay" with things in life that God never designed us to be okay with. This is not to condemn you if you are now in a dark valley or a trial. Rather, this is encouragement that you would not settle for anything less than God's perfect plan! The moment we are okay with less than His will for our life, we stop moving forward.

Being satisfied with your condition never takes you farther, whereas bending low and mourning gets answers.

No matter where you are in life, you can always go to the next level when you see your lack. Don't ever settle for where you are. There is always another step; there's always a higher plane to walk on. The Life of Christ is only available to those who need it. The Holy Spirit never forces His way into your life; He wants you to offer Him a place to stay, a place of abiding with Him, where Christ and the Holy Spirit are both welcome. This is where the nature of the dove comes in. The dove lands when it is welcome, and so the Holy Spirit wants an invitation.

Don't settle for less than His will!

55 UNABLE TO IDENTIFY WITH THE WORLD

"I do not ask that you take them out of the world, but that you keep them from the evil one. They are not of the world, just as I am not of the world. Sanctify them in the truth; your word is truth." (John 17:15-17)

Have you ever felt the pain of not being able to connect with this world system? Were there ever times in your life when you asked the question, "Why can't I be like others and have the same passions as those who love this world?" It is great to have a passion for the things God wants you to have a passion for and be excited about in life, but I believe there are going to be certain areas in your life where you wonder, "Why can't I be like others?" As Christians, we may ask, "Why can I not connect with all the social trends that are popular and loved by most who are living for self-admiration?"

All these questions should always cause our attention to focus on Christ and communion with Him. What a blessing to have a Savior to commune with! Never forget what the pit of sin felt like, where we lived in hopelessness and despair, not knowing the One who died for us.

There will be times when the path you walk with Christ will be a path of loneliness, when you are not able to connect with all the social vibes and social status; but many times this is the place where you are prepared for the ministry God has created you to fill. Don't let this dry path stop His work of performing the miracles in your heart that need to be performed.

We do not stop on a path of loneliness but we keep going, and this becomes the training ground for the next level in the Christian life. A testing ground has no purpose if we don't change and move on. We might start out in a dry desert, but we don't stay in the desert. We go from glory to glory as He changes us! We become a person completely different from the one who started out on the path.

The sad opposite situation is when people go through dry times in life and never advance any farther in their walk with Christ.

We can't identify with this world system, but we can identify with Christ and have a place of marvelous communion with the Savior of this world. The more we learn to take His Word and hide it in our hearts, the more real His life becomes within us and the more His Word brings transformation within us.

When His Word begins to take root in our heart, we will see the miraculous becoming a normal occurrence in our life.

> *"For what does it profit a man to gain the whole world and forfeit his soul? For what can a man give in return for his soul? For whosoever is ashamed of me and my words in this adulterous and sinful generation, of him will the Son of Man also be ashamed when he comes in the glory of his Father with the holy angels."* (Mark 8:36-38)

Never forget, creation is groaning for the manifestation of the sons of God. I believe many people are longing to see a man of God stand up in boldness, unashamed of Christ who died for him, even when they themselves don't have the courage to do so in public!

> *For the creation waits with eager longing for the revealing of the sons of God. (Romans 8:19)*

Just because you come in contact with people who don't have the courage to stand for Christ in public does not mean that they don't long to see that in someone else. You might have to be the first person in your group to take a stand, but you never know who will be joining you when they see your boldness for Christ.

56 THE "ABBA, FATHER!" CRY

For all who are led by the Spirit of God are sons of God. For you did not receive the spirit of slavery to fall back into fear, but you have received the Spirit of adoption as sons, by whom we cry, "Abba! Father!" The Spirit himself bears witness with our spirit that we are children of God, and if children, then heirs—heirs of God and fellow heirs with Christ, provided we suffer with him in order that we may also be glorified with him. (Romans 8:14-17)

This is one of the most glorious verses we can find in Scripture. And it shows us so clearly that we have either a spirit of slavery that falls back into fear, or the spirit of adoption as sons that brings forth an Abba, Father cry out of our heart and makes us fellow heirs with Christ.

We can know in our mind that we need to cry "Abba, Father!", but until this cry reaches the heart, it has little value to us. In today's world, we are loaded with information, and yet all the information we have seems to have little effect in transforming lives from the inside out.

We have more churches than ever before and many sermons that we say are so powerful. Yet refreshment for the human soul seems to be so hard to find. People everywhere seem to be empty, without hope, and in despair. We live in a world where sin is accepted as normal and identity seems to be lost for so many.

When we think about all the darkness attacking mankind, what is our way to a life of joy and living by His strength? We need to recognize our only Source of life. Until we see where our help comes from, we will not be much different than those who have no hope. We might be able to hold life together a little better than our neighbor (according to our opinion), but if we are not drawing from the Source, we have no true anchor for our souls.

We desperately need to understand that we can have a relationship with the One who gave His life on the cross. Jesus promised, "I will leave you a Comforter, and He will be your helper!"

We need to develop friendship with the Holy Spirit. He is the only one who can give us oil to burn in our lamp. Without this oil, we will end up being a foolish virgin, even when we say, "I've given my life to Christ." Friendship with Him is only developed through time spent with Him and a desire that craves His communion.

Unless we develop an inner longing to spend time with Him, He will never be real to us. If you have sold your life for Christ, there will come out of that a burning desire for fellowship with the Holy Spirit, a burning desire to be one with the Father as Jesus was one with the Father, and a burning desire to understand the Trinity and how the Father, Christ, and the Holy Spirit are closely connected.

Have you come to a time in your life when you can truly say, "I want to understand and spend time with the Trinity! What makes my Father's heart beat? What excites the Holy Spirit? And what is the true passion of Jesus Christ?"

One thing is clear about the Abba, Father cry: It will come bursting up from within, not as a conversation to be had with head knowledge, but from deep within as transforming waves of glory. The Abba, Father cry cannot come from head knowledge. It is found near the throne room.

57 ACCESS TO YOUR HEART

The Holy Spirit's desire is to remove all obstacles that keep you from opening up to the Father's love.

Does the Holy Spirit have access to your heart, or have you been calloused and hurt to the point where the love of the Father is only a cloudy thought? You try to understand it, but it does not make any sense.

The Bible says God is love. You might ask, "Why do I need to understand the Father's love?" One of the big things that will happen when you start walking in the understanding of His love is that you will be confident that your Father provides for you and has your best interest in mind.

When His Spirit has access to your heart, all your unnecessary struggles lose their strength and you begin to find strength and the reality of who God is. Many times, our enemy tries to keep us from entering into this place, through distraction, woundedness, unbelief, and more.

> *A heart that burns for Christ has much potential and will shake the kingdom of darkness.*

The good thing is, the enemy cannot stop the Holy Spirit coming in with power. Jesus paid for your redemption, and the Holy Spirit makes it real to you. Once the heart has been touched with His power and His flame begins to burn inside, you will begin to see why the early disciples gave their lives for the gospel.

Your heart left in your own hands becomes extremely wicked, but your heart in the hands of the Holy Spirit becomes a powerful weapon in the army of God. The enemy trembles when he sees your brokenness and surrender to your Creator. He knows he has little time, because a heart that burns for Christ has much potential and will shake the kingdom of darkness.

58 HAVE YOU MET THE SAVIOR?

"And the Father who sent me has himself borne witness about me. His voice you have never heard, his form you have never seen, and you do not have his word abiding in you, for you do not believe the one whom he has sent. You search the Scriptures

because you think that in them you have eternal life; and it is they that bear witness about me, yet you refuse to come to me that you may have life. I do not receive glory from people. But I know that you do not have the love of God within you. I have come in my Father's name, and you do not receive me. If another comes in his own name, you will receive him. How can you believe, when you receive glory from one another and do not seek the glory that comes from only God?" (John 5:37-44)

Meanwhile the disciples were urging him, saying, "Rabbi, eat." But he said to them, "I have food to eat that you do not know about." So the disciples said to one another, "Has anyone brought him something to eat?" Jesus said to them, "My food is to do the will of him who sent me and to accomplish his work." (John 4:31-34)

Jesus made one thing clear: He was here to do the will of His Father. He had set His heart to do His Father's will. Nothing was going to change His mission. What a marvelous picture of faithfulness! Is it any wonder the Holy Spirit could not leave Him in the grave?

Would it be possible to find a people who spend even half as much time seeking the will of their heavenly Father as Jesus did? Maybe get up half as early as Jesus did in the morning before anyone else is up?

Instead, it seems like we are consumed with our own goals and visions, spending so little time with Him. How can we ever know Him? How can His Word reach our heart when we don't even desire to spend a significant amount of time with Him?

We look at others and are tempted to think that somehow God shows more favor to them. Maybe we are not willing to seek God on the level they have sought after Him? A relationship is never built with a microwave mentality; it only comes about when your sail has been set and your highest goal is to know the Father and to know the deepest things in His heart.

Just as success in business takes time and effort, so I believe the one who is dedicated in his heart to seek God's face will find Him. Jesus asked, "Do you think God will give a stone when you ask for bread?" (See Matthew 7:9-11) When your eye is single and you have one goal and one purpose in life (Christ), you will find Him.

Don't think for a second that God will abandon you when you seek Him. The moment Christ becomes the King in your heart, and the Holy Spirit sees someone who has laid down everything in life, He sees someone He can work through. When Christ truly becomes the King in your heart and when you know Him and He knows you, the things that you once valued lose their grip on your soul.

Will I know when I have "sold everything" for His Kingdom? Will I know when my only goal and desire is to please Him? Will I know when the glory of God is all I'm after? These can all be tough questions, but I would rather ask them now than to think I will wait till life on earth is over—and then wish I would have.

59 THE FEAR OF THE LORD

The fear of the LORD *is the beginning of wisdom, and the knowledge of the Holy One is insight.* (Proverbs 9:10)

"All these things my hand has made, and so all these things came to be," declares the LORD. *"But this is the one to whom I will look: he who is humble and contrite in spirit and trembles at my word." (Isaiah 66:2)*

What is so valuable about the fear of the Lord? And why does God want mankind to tremble at His Word?

God made us with free will. We can choose God, or we can choose a self-life that leads to destruction.

This is why the fear of God is so powerful. The fear of God is the motivation or the steering wheel that causes us to choose our Creator.

When the fear of God is in you, you will not dare choose your own path. The fear of God will bring before your eyes the depth of your need for Him.

A generation that has lost the fear of God is such a devastating thing because if the fear of God has been lost, mankind has no pure desire for the help that comes from above. When the fear of God is lost, heaven no longer is believed to be a reality and hell is something that we don't think about. The works of the flesh don't seem to be so bad, "it's something we all struggle with." And if you have some unforgiveness lodged in your heart, it's okay, "everybody deals with it."

When the fear of God is restored, we begin to see every little act of sin as desperately wicked and in need of forgiveness. We see how one little turn in the wrong direction could take us straight to the pit of hell. When we read God's Word, the conviction of the Holy Spirit comes in a way that we can't resist it. We see how utterly lost we are if we don't receive help from above. The fear of God becomes so intense that our one goal in life is to draw from His presence.

The Bible says the fear of God is the beginning of wisdom—is it because we can only understand His goodness if we begin by fearing Him and seeing how desperately lost we are without Him? After the fear of God is established in our lives, God can show us how good He is. God longs to show us His goodness, knowing we will choose nothing different once we see it.

Today we need to ask the Holy Spirit to open our eyes to see how desperately we need Him. If we don't see our need, we will never see a reason to turn our life completely into His hands. Think about the person who is "okay" with his life as it is. Will he ever have a change of direction?

Don't settle for less than God's perfect will. He has given us free choice, and when we decide not to go farther with Him, He will not force us... but He waits on us!

60 A LIFE GIVEN TO CHRIST

[Paul] said to them… "And now, behold, I'm going to Jerusalem, constrained by the Spirit, not knowing what will happen to me there, except that the Holy Spirit testifies to me in every city that imprisonment and afflictions await me. But I do not account my life of any value nor as precious to myself, if only I may finish my course and the ministry that I received from the Lord Jesus, to testify to the gospel of the grace of God." (Acts 20:18, 22-24)

What a testimony! Most of the early disciples ended up giving their lives for the Kingdom, as their Teacher had done. In today's Western world, we know little about true persecution or execution. We become so occupied with trying to get our needs and wants met, we never learn what true giving is all about.

When it comes to giving, the first thing that comes to our mind is money. In one scene in the book of Acts, a lame beggar asked Peter and John for money, and Peter said, "I have no silver and gold, but what I do have I give to you. In the name of Jesus Christ of Nazareth, rise up and walk!" (Acts 3:6). What the disciples gave was Christ their Savior, and they did this even when it cost their life's blood.

When a man discovers Christ, he begins to understand the gospel is much more than earthly riches. Christ has got to be our answer for every need we come in contact with. It is great to give when there are financial needs, but I wonder sometimes where we think the answer lies. Do we look to Him first, or are we convinced money holds more power than Christ?

We have been trained to think that our answer is in earthly substance rather than in the King who died on the cross for all mankind. The Great Awakening that is coming, I believe, will be when man recognizes Christ has more power than anything man can ever produce.

The Bible says the streets of Heaven are paved with gold. In Heaven, gold—the thing we value so much—is walked on! The true glory will be the Throne Room, where the Father, Christ, and the Holy Spirit are.

The Apostle Paul understood his mission, and even though the Holy Spirit told him it was going to be rough, he did not hold back. He did it all for the name of Christ. In today's world, most of us are looking for an easy life, a life where we can say we have finally "arrived." But Paul understood that it was in his greatest need, he became his strongest.

There is no way around it. The time will come when our lives will be spent, and they will either be spent on our own interests or on Christ. He spent everything He had for us. The only way we can truly call this "Christianity" is if we are willing to spend it all for Him.

61 SAVED BY GRACE

For by grace you have been saved through faith. And this is not your own doing; it is the gift of God. (Ephesians 2:8)

How easy it is to be saved by grace and yet so quickly fall back into thinking it is through my own piety that I am kept connected to Christ. When the cares of life come knocking on our door and anxiety wants a grip on the heart, and we forget Christ saved us and think we must save ourselves! And whenever we find the breakthrough that we've been looking for, the temptation will still be to think *we* must keep ourselves saved. Some of your greatest victories will be followed by the temptation to think that *you* can keep yourself in this position.

Yet He says, "I have saved you, and I will keep you saved." It sounds so simple, yet this is what so many of us are tempted with, and we become overwhelmed with the weight that life wants to bring against us. Remember, you have been saved by grace, and you need to stay saved by grace!

God's Word says we have been saved by grace through faith. The enemy attempts to discourage our faith so that the grace of His strength cannot have its full effect on us.

Grace is His strength in exchange for mine! A glorious experience, to exchange our strength for His! When "life" happens, this is the most vital thing to put into action. Then it is no longer my strength but His. It is no longer I, but Christ in me. This is the only way we can have true rest, the only way we can ever know the fullness of who He is.

I believe this is why the Bible says:

> And [Jesus] said, "Truly, I say to you, unless you turn and become like children, you will never enter the kingdom of heaven. Whoever humbles himself like this child is the greatest in the kingdom of heaven." (Matthew 18:3-4)

A child has no problem resting in his father's strength. Our problem as adults is our thinking that we are responsible for the victories in our life, when in reality, we are responsible for resting in Him. A child has no problem being humble enough to take refuge and comfort in the strength of his father. We adults become so stiff-necked and proud, thinking, I am my own source!

Think about your natural body; when you are sick, the doctor will tell you what you need is rest. It is no different in your spiritual walk with Christ. When we learn to rest in Him, we regain vitality and strength.

Life becomes complicated, but the gospel never does. If you have come to a place where your strength has been zapped, remember that His grace brings an overflow of strength and life.

62 UNNECESSARY WEIGHTS, DISTRACTING TRIALS

How many unnecessary weights we carry that we were never meant to bear!

Many things come against us to distract and discourage. We think we are responsible for unnecessary burdens, or we have tendencies in our personalities that bring conflict in relationships. The enemy's goal is to bring distraction and burdens that take us away from knowing the fullness of who God is and His plan for our life.

In many testimonies of those who have had near-death experiences, one thing many have testified is that when they leave their body, everything becomes crystal clear and they feel light. When they come back into their body, they say they feel choked down and their body becomes heavy. Many comment on how uncertain life on earth is. In the language of eternity, people know things without being told. It's a land of knowing; nobody has to tell you.

So many things about our life here on this planet are uncertain, and we become bogged down with unnecessary weights. We find ourselves saying, "If only I knew what the answer was, I could do something about it." Uncertainty and questions we never seem to find answers for can be so painful in this life. Things would be better, it seems, if we only knew the full story.

We were designed to live on trust and faith whenever we come into a situation where there are no clear answers. Jesus said, "I will send you a helper, the Holy Spirit." The deeper we go into relationship with the Spirit and the more we learn to hear His voice, the more He empowers us to trust our Maker and have faith.

Jesus' life was built on a relationship with his Father and a close relationship with the Holy Spirit. Our enemy tries his best to keep us from this same relationship. Mankind was born into sin and things come against us at a young age, and many times it seems like the devil's plan is too successful. But the moment our heart fully turns to the Lord and salvation enters our spirit and soul, the Holy Spirit has a foundation to begin to speak to us.

Even then, even after this relationship with Christ is established, we are challenged by these distractions and weights designed by the devil to distract us from the voice of the Holy Spirit. The devil doesn't care how he does it; all he wants to do is keep us from understanding and comprehending the full knowledge of God in all wisdom.

Our Creator has designed a path for us to walk, where our relationship with Him is real. When we become saturated in who He is, He clearly shows us unnecessary weights that are bogging us down. On this path and in relationship with Him, there *is* a power to break free from distractions and burdens.

There is no trial and no weight that the power of Heaven is not able to take off our life. It might look hopeless. It might seem like there is no answer. But is your situation any worse than what the disciples experienced on those days between the crucifixion of their Messiah and their discovery of the empty tomb? Did they have any hope for Him to be resurrected? Peter said, "I'm going fishing." However, the Holy Spirit had other plans. He is the resurrection and the life! The Spirit will do what He was sent to do, even when it looks like all hope is lost.

We see this same thing in the life of Moses; after he killed an Egyptian, he spent 40 years in the wilderness being made by God. The ministry of Jesus did not begin until the age of 30. John the Baptist was a voice crying in the wilderness. Abraham received his promise at nearly 100 years of age. Noah took about 120 years to build the ark. Even when we've been in a dry state for a long time, the Spirit is still developing a child of God.

Whenever things are uncertain and it seems like nothing is happening, it is vital that we learn to endure and to continue doing what is just and right, knowing that one day all our questions will be answered.

Whether a breakthrough comes in 3 days or 120 years, if our lives are surrendered to Christ and we live by His righteousness, breakthrough will come, in His time! In His Word, we read that one day with the Lord is as a thousand years and a thousand years as one day. Time is no issue to God as He accomplishes His plan and purposes.

63 HIS NAME GLORIFIED

"Now is my soul troubled. And what shall I say? 'Father, save me from this hour'? But for this purpose I have come to this hour. Father, glorify your name." Then a voice came from heaven: "I have glorified it, and I will glorify it again." The crowd that stood there and heard it said that it had thundered. Others said, "An angel has spoken to him." Jesus answered, "This voice has come for your sake, not mine. Now is the judgment of this world; now will the ruler of this world be cast out. And I, when I am lifted up from the earth, will draw all people to myself." (John 12:27-32)

Jesus came to a crossroads. His soul was troubled, and He began to question if He should ask the Father to save Him from what He knew was ahead (John 12:27). But then He answered His own question: "For this purpose I have come to this hour." In the garden before the crucifixion, Peter tried to defend his teacher when they came to arrest Jesus, but Jesus' question to Peter was, "Shall I not drink the cup that is set before me?"

The choice Jesus made was, "Father, glorify Your name!" Right after this public decision, Heaven opened up and God's voice had an impact. And because of His decision to be obedient for the glory of the Father, our story in life now has so much potential.

I believe if we make this same statement from deep within our heart— even when our soul is troubled—Heaven will speak. You might be misunderstood, like those with Jesus who thought God's voice was thunder or an angel. But the glory of it is—Heaven spoke!

The best choice we will ever make is to repeat after Jesus, "Father, glorify Your name!" We too come to many crossroads in life where we have the opportunity to repeat this wonderful and glorious prayer that Jesus prayed when He made the decision to follow through with His Father's plan for His life.

When our back is to the wall and it seems like there's nowhere else to turn, this can be a perfect time for the manifested glory of God. We need a miracle because a solution or help is naturally impossible. We desperately need a change of direction—a breakthrough. We all like testimonies of the miraculous, but we don't enjoy being in that situation; and from a natural standpoint, this prayer asking God to glorify *His* name will look like the wrong response. But the glory of this is—God is ready to pour out supernatural strength on our situation!

Father, glorify Your name!

64 A BLAMELESS WALK, A COVENANT ESTABLISHED

If we look at how God established a covenant with His people in the first part of Genesis, we can see it all began with a generation.

> *To Seth also a son was born... At that time people began to call upon the name of the LORD. (Genesis 4:26)*

> *Enoch walked with God... All the days of Enoch were 365 years. Enoch walked with God, and he was not, for God took him. (Genesis 5:22-24)*

> *But Noah found favor in the eyes of the LORD... Noah was a righteous man, blameless in his generation. Noah walked with God. (Genesis 6:8-9)*

When Abram was ninety-nine years old the LORD appeared to Abram and said to him, "I am God Almighty; walk before me, and be blameless, that I may make my covenant between me and you, and may multiply you greatly. And I will establish my covenant between me and you and your offspring after you throughout their generations for an everlasting covenant, to be God to you and to your offspring after you."
(Genesis 17:1-2, 7-8)

Why did God have His eye on this generation? This was a generation who began to call on the name of the Lord, a generation who had a blameless walk; a generation who walked with God; a generation who stood for the righteousness of the King. This generation sought God and established a family line of men who found favor in God's eyes, leading to God's everlasting covenant with them.

Can the same be said of us? Are we a generation in which His covenant can be established? Do we stand for righteousness no matter the cost? Do we walk in a place where He can show himself strong? Do we walk blameless with God?

When God appeared to Abram, His message was, "Walk before me blameless so that I might establish my covenant with you." Was this only for Abram, or is this also for us? I believe God's word to us is the same as His word to Abram. The message was and still is: "Walk before me blameless!"

What is a blameless walk? If we are to have an effect wherever we go, it must be through a blameless walk, a walk where our only intention is for His name to be glorified.

A characteristic of a blameless walk is that we don't respond out of feelings or emotions when we get hit with unjust actions. Many times Jesus could have opened His mouth in the presence of His accusers, but He chose confidence in His heavenly Father.

When we are treated unjustly, we often fail to walk blamelessly and do not follow Jesus' example. Our problem is that we often have a short-term plan and mindset. The way we live will dramatically change when we recognize and imitate the farmer who plants a seed and then walks away from it and lets it begin its growing process. Almost always, sin is the fruit of a short-term mindset when we want quick results and we're not willing to wait with patience, knowing justice will win at the end. Even if it takes a hundred years for justice to come around, it's better to be patient and have end results that bring satisfaction.

How powerful when a man truly has confidence in the fact that righteousness and justice will always prevail!

65 THE LEAST OF ALL SEEDS AND SMALL IMPRESSIONS

He put another parable before them, saying, "The kingdom of heaven is like a grain of mustard seed that a man took and sowed in his field. It is the smallest of all seeds, but when it has grown it is larger than all the garden plants and becomes a tree, so that the birds of the air come and make nests in its branches."
(Matthew 13:31-32)

For who has despised the day of small things? But these seven will be glad when they see the plumb line in the hand of Zerubbabel—these are the eyes of the LORD, which range to and fro throughout the earth. (Zechariah 4:10 NASB1995)

And your ears shall hear a word behind you, saying, "This is the way, walk in it," when you turn to the right or when you turn to the left. (Isaiah 30:21)

How many times do we miss God's voice because we are expecting a big booming encounter when instead God is trying to get our attention with impressions in our ears small enough to be easily missed? We look for the grand experiences to transform our lives, failing to understand that many times His words come in a still, small voice so quiet that most people miss it.

We spend our entire life looking for a miracle on the top shelf when God says, "I've put it on the bottom shelf where even a child can reach it!" Our enemy likes to work alongside human nature, pulling us so easily into the deception that says anything from a higher power must be complicated and hard to get. When we think

The day we learn to hear His voice and yield to the small impressions He lays on our heart is the day we begin to move forward in our walk with Christ.

according to the natural man, a miracle becomes complicated and a breakthrough almost unattainable. The natural man complicates the simplest matters, but the man who walks in the Spirit does not allow the natural man to make the final decision.

The day we learn to hear His voice and yield to the small impressions He lays on our heart is the day we begin to move forward in our walk with Christ. His quiet, soft voice has potential strong enough to change the direction of our life's path.

Child of God, do not despise small beginnings, for this is where He starts in our lives. Keep sowing seeds of righteousness, knowing that your day of harvest is coming. Jesus is our perfect example. He began in a manger, but today He is Savior of the world.

66 TRUST IN GOD

How easy it is to begin to put our confidence in man! However, there is only One who can be trusted with our entire life. There is only One who paid for your salvation with His own life's blood. There is only One who was brave enough to lay His life on a cross and became the perfect sacrifice. In Him we can rest assured that every area of our life is covered, and only in Him can our soul find complete rest.

Many times we hear the word *faith* and we think of some supernatural ability to receive salvation and miracles—and rightly so—but faith also needs to *trust* Him. Trust is a powerful word, indicating that our confidence is in Him. How much confidence and trust do I have in my God when it comes to everyday life?

In this life we will face many uncertainties, and our hearts need to trust Him. Regardless what comes against us, our confidence must be in Him. The devil would love for us to have confidence in some unstable source, other people or some earthly substance. He knows when that source fails (and it will) he has an opportunity to shake us to the core. But whenever we have our heart set to trust in God's Word, there is nothing that can shake us to the point we lose our salvation.

Jesus was asleep in a boat with His disciples when a storm threatened to sink them.

> *And they went and woke him, saying, "Master, Master, we are perishing!" And he awoke and rebuked the wind and the raging waves, and they ceased, and there was a calm. He said to them, "Where is your faith?" (Luke 8:24-25)*

They believed they were perishing. While He was in the boat with them! The one who has faith will learn to trust in his God and will find rest while everyone else sees utter destruction. We cannot let what is happening around us bring destruction inside us.

> *Great peace have those who love your law; nothing can make them stumble. (Psalm 119:165)*

His Word is an anchor that will hold us fast and bring a stability to our inner being. It is vital that our heart is touched by His Word; when this takes place, we learn to trust more and more, and we find a place of rest. His peace comes in and floods our soul. Faith and trust will go hand-in-hand so that the storm around us does not destroy us.

Jesus said, "Trust me, and trust God" (John 14:1) and "My peace I give to you" (John 14:27). When we learn to trust Him, we can be a green plant in a dry desert.

"Blessed is the man who trusts in the LORD, whose trust is the LORD. He is like a tree planted by water, that sends out its roots by the stream, and does not fear when heat comes, for its leaves remain green, and is not anxious in the year of drought, for it does not cease to bear fruit." (Jeremiah 17:7-8)

67 A DESIRE FOR GOD

For it is God who works in you, both to will and to work for his good pleasure. (Philippians 2:13)

"No one can come to me unless the Father who sent me draws him. And I will raise him up in the last day." (John 6:44)

Who are we to think somehow our desire for God comes because of something we have done or who we are? Unless He draws us to Himself, how can our hearts ever desire Him? He puts a desire within us in order to bring us to Himself. This fact alone should bring the fear of God into our hearts, because how easy it is for us to forget from whence we came.

We see this when Moses led the children of Israel in the wilderness.

But they soon forgot his works; they did not wait for his counsel. But they had a wanton craving in the wilderness, and put God to the test in the desert; he gave them what they asked, but sent a wasting disease among them.

Then they despised the pleasant land, having no faith in his promise. They murmured in their tents, and did not obey the voice of the LORD. (Psalm 106:13-15, 24-25)

We come to dry times in our lives, and it is only by His mercy and grace that we come back out and find again a place of strength and refreshment. Our souls need Him more than anything else! There is no substitute for the Master of our soul.

He knew there would be times of drought, times of disappointment. Times of not knowing what my next step in life is.

> *Be patient, therefore, brothers, until the coming of the Lord. See how the farmer waits for the precious fruit of the earth, being patient about it, until it receives the early and late rains. (James 5:7)*

God's will for our life is for us to trust in Him for times of refreshing, for times when His Spirit is real to us. As the farmer waits for the fruit of the earth, for the early and late rains to have their effect on the crop, so we need to be patient, knowing rain is coming.

Another place we read:

> *Where shall I go from your Spirit? Or where shall I flee from your presence? If I ascend to heaven, you are there! If I make my bed in Sheol, you are there! If I take the wings of the morning and dwell in the uttermost parts of the sea, even there your hand shall lead me, and your right hand shall hold me. (Psalm 139:7-10)*

We can easily forget that God is with us, but He is faithful regardless of our feelings or circumstances. God is so much better than man, and His ways are much higher than our ways. His love never fails. His presence goes with us wherever we go. Even in the darkest pit He will find us; we are not hidden from His eye. In the midst of a drought, He knows when the rain is coming.

We may be tempted to think God has forgotten, but He says, "I will never leave you nor forsake you!"

68 A CRY FOR HIS RIGHTEOUSNESS

How much time do we spend crying out for His righteousness to be restored on Earth?

We can be consumed with our own personal needs rather than glorifying Christ; then Christ cannot be seen in our lives and His righteousness ends up being something that we find as a strange subject.

But the more God's people desire to hear their Creator's voice, the more a cry for His righteousness comes forth.

The world will think it's strange that our utmost concern is for His righteousness to be restored, and this passion will be considered a foolish one. This can be a difficult place to walk.

Our only chance to convince a lost and dying world to seek after something that looks so foolish to the natural eye is for us to walk in a place where His joy is written on our faces. Consider Stephen in the early church; as he was on trial and falsely accused before the religious rulers, the Bible says his face looked like the face of an angel. It makes one wonder how many souls were saved out of this perfect reflection of Christ?

A magnified Christ is much better than a magnified self. How can we show who He is more clearly to those around us? This is not always done through words, because sometimes the loudest voice is the one that is felt and not spoken.

Unless we become a city on a hill and a lamp lighting the house, why should the world think that we have any answers?

How glorious to consider that we can shine for Christ no matter our social status or degree of education. His mercy has made a way for us to be His effective witness, a way not based on any natural ability. The world system says "If you're not naturally gifted, we have no use for you." The Holy Spirit only asks you to be available, and then He will qualify you and make you a part of the work of Heaven.

The cry from a child of God for His righteousness to be restored is a cry for every wrong thing to be made right. We need never be satisfied with anything less than His will fulfilled on this earth. At the end, righteousness *will* be restored and justice *will* be served. Saint of God, you need not fear. Keep sowing seeds of righteousness, knowing planted seeds will grow and you will have a harvest. It's only a matter of time!

69 A SATISFIED SOUL

He makes me lie down in green pastures. He leads me beside still waters. He restores my soul. He leads me in the paths of righteousness for his name's sake. (Psalm 23:2-3)

Down through history, mankind has tried to fill the gap in his soul with so many things—things that have left his soul even more empty than when he began his search for meaning and fulfillment.

Oh, that we come to the place where we understand there is only One who can fill that inner void! There is only One who can give water to drink so that we never thirst again. Any other water will not satisfy; any water outside of the real Water of Life will only increase a thirst that cannot be quenched.

My soul will be satisfied as with fat and rich food, and my mouth will praise you with joyful lips. (Psalm 63:5)

We can point our fingers at drug addicts, but we fail to realize they have an addiction because they are thirsty and trying to fill a void that only Christ can fill. And yet, if we as born-again believers don't trust in Christ for our every need in life, we are doing the same thing in a more disguised way. A soul seeking satisfaction outside of Christ is a soul that will never find true rest until there is a change of direction.

Whenever we try to fill a void with anything outside of Christ, somebody will end up wounded, because the foundation of this is self-determination and greed. Even though we dress it up and make it look nice, the foundation will always be wrong.

There is only One who can satisfy; there is only One who knows how to heal the great gap in the soul of man. Christ dealt with every void that mankind will ever know. His love will be the only satisfaction mankind will ever meet. Only in His presence will there be a complete restoration of things lost.

An attitude of trust must bring complete and total dependence on Him, knowing we can walk with Him in a place of confidence and faith, resulting in a satisfied soul.

70 DIRECTION AND PRESSURE

Many times we ask God to give us direction—and then we experience extreme difficulty and we wonder why.

At the birth of Jesus, angels announced a Savior had been born and part of their message was "Peace on earth!" Shouldn't there have been automatic peace on earth? But the reality was that as soon as the Baby was born, the enemy was after Him, determined to end His life. Every time God does something out of the ordinary, it seems as though there is always extreme pressure that opposes what He is doing.

The words of Jesus were,

> *"Do not think that I have come to bring peace to the earth. I have not come to bring peace, but a sword. For I have come to set a man against his father, and a daughter against her mother, and a*

daughter-in-law against her mother-in-law. A person's enemies will be those of his own household." (Matthew 10:34-36)

Whenever light enters a place of darkness, there will always be resistance! We would love to think that all people would be excited and eager for light to enter and illuminate areas in their lives that need direction, but reality can be quite the opposite.

We look at the condition of the world today and we know we are getting close to the return of Christ. Shouldn't the coming of the Prince of Peace be a time when turmoil ceases and victory becomes obvious? Many times, we misunderstand; before an actual birth, there will be times of intense pressure and we'll wonder, "Is it all going to be okay?"

This is also true in our personal lives: when we need direction, there will often be pressure and resistance. The further we go with God, the more we begin to understand that pressure may be necessary in order for direction to come. Maturity brings us to a place where we embrace the pressure, knowing that God uses it for our benefit. Understanding this will set us free in so many different ways; whenever we pray for an answer and the pressure begins to rise, we can clearly see God at work.

Before Jesus Christ paid for the sins of the whole world, He came under pressure so severe that He began to sweat drops of blood in the Garden. And on the cross, He went through such extreme suffering that it seemed like His Father in Heaven had forsaken Him. No other man ever went through the depth of suffering He bore. And no other man paid for the sins of the whole world in one day!

Embrace the difficulty. Embrace the pressure. Embrace mistreatment. The early church understood this, and they became so effective that today we can read many testimonies in the biblical accounts. Jesus endured the cross for the joy that was set before Him. The greatest rewards, I believe, are for those who give their lives for the gospel. They can do this only because they understand the glory that is on the other side.

It's hard to embrace difficulty when we have comfort uppermost in mind. It's hard to embrace pressure when we have ease as our goal. It's hard to embrace mistreatment when our lives desire the approval of man. Ask for direction, and then embrace how He wants to handle it. Because answered prayers don't always look like what you expect.

71 ENDURING AFFLICTION

For this is the will of God, that by doing good you should put to silence the ignorance of foolish people. (1 Peter 2:15)

For what credit is it if, when you sin and are beaten for it, you endure? But if when you do good and suffer for it you endure, this is a gracious thing in the sight of God. For to this you have been called, because Christ also suffered for you, leaving you an example, so that you might follow in his steps. He committed no sin, neither was deceit found in his mouth. When he was reviled, he did not revile in return; when he suffered, he did not threaten, but continued entrusting himself to him who judges justly. (1 Peter 2:20-23)

Jesus' way of dealing with opposition and conflict was so pure and so holy even His enemies could not bring anything against Him in an honest way. He had a blameless walk, and I believe this is one of the main reasons they could not stand Him. He was too straightforward, too honest; He spoke nothing in secret. There was no hypocrisy anywhere in His life. When you met Him, what you saw is what you got. On the night He stood on trial before the high priest, one of His statements was,

Jesus answered him, "I have spoken openly to the world. I have always taught in synagogues and in the temple, where all Jews come together. I have said nothing in secret." (John 18:20)

Think about all the things done in secret. The day is coming for the covers to be taken off and all the things in darkness will be brought to light. All the kings and the leaders of this world will face an uncovering that will shake the foundation of this world.

Jesus operated in divine wisdom and divine understanding. But one of the things that gets my attention is that He was so honest and so straightforward in His conversations that, I believe, it became extremely painful for those who were hiding their sin. Those who had an agenda were stripped of their power. And the only thing they knew to do about it was to crucify Him. Even in this, the cry came forth, "Father, forgive them! They don't know what they're doing."

Our walk needs to be no different because He was the perfect example and He left us with the Holy Spirit, to do greater works than even what He had done. Our top priority should be to walk in a place of holiness and purity so that those around us will have to make a decision: Will I stand for righteousness and holiness or will I fight against the God of Heaven, Creator of all?

72 A DESIRE

Our desire for God is part of the chariot that takes us into His presence.

A desire is a hunger to come before Him, and if we lack this deep inner longing, He cannot guide our life. He must be the last thing we think about when we lie down at night and the first thing that comes to mind when we wake up in the morning.

If this longing to be in His presence becomes a part of our life, the Holy Spirit will speak to us in the most astounding and real way. When our eye becomes single and our heart is set on Him, He guides our life in a way that was never possible before. Life is no longer about what we can get, but rather about how His name can be magnified.

Down through history, those who were used by God the most were those who refused to love anything more than Him. Those who were in love with Him, those who longed for the day when they would see Him face to face. If we are to be the bride of Christ, then our deepest desire must be for the wedding day that is coming soon.

God needs our full attention in order to perform His Kingdom in our lives. This is why the distraction our enemy uses against us is one of his deadliest weapons. If he can get our attention and consume our lives with something other than Christ, then our lives are in danger of decay and destruction and will not glorify Christ.

This is why the Bible says He gives you the desires of your heart, because a desire is what He uses to take us where we should go. When we desire all the distractions of this world, that desire takes us to corruption and the god of this world. When we desire God, it brings us to Himself and His Kingdom!

73 PERSONAL REVELATION: OIL IN YOUR LAMP

"Then the kingdom of heaven will be like ten virgins who took their lamps and went to meet the bridegroom. Five of them were foolish, and five were wise. For when the foolish took their lamps, they took no oil with them." (Matthew 25:1-3)

One of the greatest needs today is for Christians to experience Christ for themselves.

Salvation is personal and hearing His voice is personal. We cannot depend on someone else's revelation of Christ or someone else's intimacy with the Holy Spirit. What someone else has experienced will never be enough in our own times of difficulty or testing—or at the return of Christ! There is no pastor or evangelist strong enough to stand for you or me after the sum total of our lives on earth has been written.

Notice in the parable Jesus gave in Matthew 25 that all of the ten were virgins. Could we say they were all born-again Christians? Five of them were wise and recognized their need for oil, while the other five were foolish and took their lamps but no extra oil. If they would have recognized how desperately they would need oil, they would have been welcomed in to the wedding feast instead of having the door shut in their faces.

We can have all the doctrine correct and yet be devastated at the end because we simply do not recognize our need for oil. How devastated many people will be at the end because they never recognized their need for oil while everything seemed to be going okay in life. When times are going great, this is the time to recognize our need for Christ and the Holy Spirit. Too many people wait to seek after God until they come to a difficult place in life and then ask for oil from someone else rather than from the true source.

It is best to seek Him and recognize our need before a desperate situation arises. Today is the day of salvation. The best time to build a relationship is today. The reality is that we do have a desperate need every day whether we recognize it or not. Those who see how desperately they need Him every day will be buying oil in good times.

The world will think you are foolish to be desperate for God in good times, but they have their eyes blinded to the fact that every man and woman will one day appear before the Creator of this world.

> *The fear of the LORD is the beginning of wisdom, and the knowledge of the Holy One is insight. If you are wise, you are wise for yourself; if you scoff, you alone will bear it.*
> *(Proverbs 9:10, 12)*

Maybe we need to ask our Helper to baptize us in the fear of the Lord, for this is the beginning of wisdom. Without the fear of the Lord, without seeing our desperate need, we become blinded to the fact that every minute counts. We don't have time to waste; it's only foolish to think we do.

74 SHEEP OR GOAT

"When the Son of Man comes in his glory, and all the angels with him, then he will sit on his glorious throne. Before him will be gathered all the nations, and he will separate people one from another as a shepherd separates the sheep from the goats. And he will place the sheep on his right, but the goats on the left." Then the King will say to those on his right, 'Come, you who are blessed by my Father, inherit the kingdom prepared for you from the foundation of the world.' Then he will say to those on his left, 'Depart from me, you cursed, into the eternal fire prepared for the devil and his angels.'" (Matthew 25:31-34, 41)

Why can goats not hear the voice of the Shepherd? The nature of a goat is to push his way through no matter what obstacle he comes up against. He is so focused on his own desires that his mind cannot take the time to think about the needs around him. In other words, it doesn't matter who he hurts or who is hurting as long as he gets what he wants.

In contrast, a sheep is so dependent on the Shepherd that his ears have become sensitive. He is no longer dependent on pushing but rather on being led by his Shepherd's voice.

To the eyes of the natural man, the goat is many times the one who appears to be brilliant. The goat has the ability to do things on his own, whereas the sheep is dependent on the One who knows all things. Left on their own, the goat will appear to go much farther than the sheep, but once the sheep hears the Shepherd's voice, there can be no comparison! The Shepherd's voice will take you places that you have no chance of going while you're depending on your own ability.

The Shepherd knows all things; He has been around long before the sheep and the goat. If only the goat would stop and consider that perhaps the Shepherd knows what is best. But he has made up his mind. "I will do what I can, I will go where I want. Besides, I am wise; I have done it for many years. What's the point of depending on the Shepherd when it seems like life is going great?"

The goat desires his own glory, but the sheep knows the Son of Man will appear with His glory, and he would rather be patient and find Christ as his dearest friend and Savior than to seek his own glory now.

Matthew 25 is speaking about final judgment, but I believe this is also true in our current time. Even at this moment, people are gathered before Him and current situations are being documented in the books of Heaven.

Your life is being recorded, so regardless what cup gets handed to you, you can trust in your God, because when the Son of Man returns in His glory, all people will be gathered before Him; and only those who find themselves at His right hand will hear the words, "Come, you who are blessed, and inherit the Kingdom!"

75 CHRIST GLORIFIED

And beginning with Moses and all the Prophets, he interpreted to them in all the Scriptures the things concerning himself... And their eyes were opened, and they recognized him. Then he opened their minds to understand the Scriptures... (Luke 24:27, 31, 45)

Has the veil been taken from your eyes that you can see who Christ is? Luke's account says that the risen, glorified Christ opened their minds to understand all the Scriptures about Him. Today we have the Holy Spirit, and He has the ability to open our minds to the reality of Christ.

The Holy Spirit can do in a second what you have strived for your whole life. It's not the striving that counts; it's only revelation by the power of the Holy Spirit that will reveal Christ and the deep things from the heart of God.

Has your heart been opened to the revelation of Jesus Christ? We know so many things in our heads, but what about knowing Christ from the heart?

76 WHEN GOD APPEARS TO THE BLAMELESS

We all desire answers to the complicated questions in our lives. Will God come to us and speak to us in the midst of our difficulty as He did in Bible accounts?

Job's difficulties and questions were great, and we can read how God came to him:

> Job 38:1 and again in 40:6 - Then the LORD answered Job out of the whirlwind and said...

In Genesis we read about the Lord appearing to Abram:

> Genesis 17:1 - When Abram was 99 years old the LORD appeared to Abram and said to him...

> Genesis 18:1 - And the LORD appeared to him by the oaks of Mamre, as he sat at the door of his tent In the heat of the day.

The Lord came to Samuel, calling his name:

> 1 Samuel 3:10 - And the LORD came and stood calling as at other times, "Samuel! Samuel!" And Samuel said, "Speak, for your servant hears."

God spoke to Moses out of a burning bush (and the subsequent conversations between the Lord and Moses throughout Exodus are quite extensive):

> Exodus 3:2 - And the angel of the LORD appeared to him in a flame of fire out of the midst of the bush.

Noah walked with God, and God spoke with him:

> Genesis 6:9 - Noah was a righteous man, blameless in his generation. Noah walked with God.

> Genesis 7:1 - Then the Lord said to Noah, go into the ark..

> Genesis 8:15 - Then God said to Noah...

> Genesis 9:1 - And God blessed Noah and his sons and said to them...

Those are only a few accounts in the Old Testament of God speaking to His people. Then we go to the New Testament, starting with Jesus (and all those with Him):

> Matthew 3:16-17 – And when Jesus was baptized... behold a voice from Heaven said...

> Matthew 17:5 – He [Jesus] was still speaking when... a voice from the cloud said...

We read about Saul, on his way to Damascus:

> Acts 9:3-4 – Suddenly a light from heaven shown around him. And falling to the ground he heard a voice saying to him...

When the apostles were arrested and put in prison:

> Acts 5:19 - But during the night an angel of the Lord opened the prison doors and brought them out, and said...

Peter, rescued from prison:

> Acts 12:7, 8 - And behold, an angel of the Lord stood next to him, and a light shown in the cell... And the angel said to him...

And then we could add the many accounts of Jesus appearing to His disciples after He arose from the grave, as many as 500 at one time (see 1 Corinthians 15:6).

Will God do the miraculous and speak to us in our day?

We can be either lost in a pit of unbelief and hopelessness, or we can be of those who recognize how great a need we have and choose to turn our hearts to Him for every answer in our lives. It is many times when we can see no options and our heart cries out to Him for answers that we see the hand of the Lord in our life and hear His voice speaking to us.

One thing that keeps many from experiencing more of God is that in this modern day we live in, the world offers so many options. The enemy whispers that If God doesn't come through, we can always turn to the world for help.

Our eyes need to be opened to see what is true help. His Word says "the truth will set you free," and we will only turn to God when we see clearly Who is our source of true help and what is only a crutch that props us up temporarily.

Where are you looking for help?

> *I lift my eyes to the hills. From where does my help come? My help comes from the LORD, who made heaven and earth. (Psalm 121:1-2)*

77 GROWING UP INTO CHRIST

> *But grow in the grace and knowledge of our Lord and Savior Jesus Christ. To him be the glory both now and to the day of eternity. Amen. (2 Peter 3:18)*

Growing up in Christ will take endurance and patience, with long-suffering. It doesn't happen overnight.

It's okay to be in a growing process. There will be times when we think we've been at the same place for way too long. We need to remember that growing takes patience. God knows what He is building, and we need to trust the process. As we grow up in the knowledge of our Lord and Savior Jesus Christ, it is important that we learn to be at peace even at times we think we're at a standstill.

For you know that the testing of your faith produces steadfastness. And let steadfastness have its full effect, that you may be perfect and complete, lacking nothing. (James 1:3-4)

> *God knows what He is building, and we need to trust the process.*

God is more concerned about the end product than He is about making sure you are satisfied with the process. Why does the process need to be so complex? This can be one of the most difficult things in life to understand. There are many seasons in life, and we don't need to understand every detail about the seasons, but what will help us tremendously is understanding that God is in the building business, and He knows what makes the strongest and the best building.

He has seen those who built their life on sand, and He has seen those who built their life on the rock, Christ Jesus. The ones who built their life on Christ have faced many difficulties and so have the ones who built their life on sand. The difference is the end result!

After your life has been written, what will be left? Has His Kingdom been established in your life? Has His name been glorified? Have you become a useful vessel? Was Christ the one who was reflected in your everyday life?

Our goal is to grow up in the knowledge of Christ and have a walk that can be called a blameless walk. Not blameless because of our own perfection, but blameless because of a perfect reflection of who Christ is in us. When there is a failure, when there are thoughts of defeat, at the end of it, Christ is still our righteousness.

We tend to see our shortcomings, but with Christ as our righteousness, yielded to Him, the eyes of our Father will see no fault in us. All He sees is Jesus! He is satisfied with the work of His Son. And we need to be satisfied with the work of Christ. This is our only hope. Be at peace.

Therefore, beloved, since you are waiting for these, be diligent to be found by him without spot or blemish, and at peace.
(2 Peter 3:14)

78 CONVERSATION IN HEAVEN

Christ not only removed all our sins, but at this moment He is before our Father in Heaven, interceding for us. If we could only hear this conversation, it would dramatically change the way we think about our weaknesses and shortcomings.

I wonder sometimes what the conversation between Christ and the Father sounds like, concerning the saints.

"Father, you can't hold it against them. I paid for every sin they ever committed and every sin they will ever commit. From the vilest sinner to the purest saint—there is no difference—I paid the price. Let them go free. Let the blood that I gave cleanse and save them from destruction.

"I remember the weight of their sin. I remember the agony in the garden when I sweat drops of blood. I remember when all my disciples fled for their life. I remember the crown of thorns, the whip lashing my back, the nails going through my hands.

"I remember the moment I cried out and asked why You had forsaken me.

"Father, I know You were satisfied when I cried 'It is finished!' and slipped into the dark lonely grave, when those around me thought they would never see me again. I know that was enough.

"Let them go free!"

79 FLAWED TO PURE AND COMPLETE

For we all stumble in many ways. And if anyone does not stumble in what he says, he is a perfect man, able also to bridle his whole body. (James 3:2)

Have you ever spoken words and then wished you could go back and hit the delete button? We often find ourselves tempted to speak in order to satisfy some emotional void, but the moment we speak out the words, we know they never should have been said.

The pain and agony of words that never should have been spoken!

However, this gives us an opportunity to go back and examine everything that led up to this act. Maybe the words came forth from pure ignorance, not knowing any better; or maybe they were birthed out of some character flaw?

God knows! Our Maker sees our weakness and He has the ability to purify our motives.

Whether our flaws are small or great, the Holy Spirit is here to correct them and bring every person to a place of purity and integrity and completeness, lacking nothing. Our job is to turn to Him and allow Him to bring us to this absolute integrity and into a walk that is blameless.

What is *blameless*? James says that when we don't stumble with our words, we have reached a place where we are able to guide our whole body.

Sometimes this can be a hard lesson to learn. Every once in a while, we open our mouths and something comes out and we ask, *Where did that come from? I had no idea that it was still there!* Sin will always find its way out through the tongue, whether it's now or later. It's not worth trying to hide any sin, small or great.

This is not a time to be discouraged but a time to cry out to Him and ask Him to change the root of those words. He is the King of all righteousness, the King of integrity. He has the authority to forgive sins. All He needs from us is confession out of a heart that believes in His goodness, because when He grants repentance, our lives are changed.

Our goal is not simply to control our words, but to have a walk such that whenever we open our mouth, integrity and purity are felt by those around us!

> *There is hope for the man*
> *who has all intentions of*
> *allowing Christ to deal with his life*
> *and hide nothing.*

80 THE APPEARING OF CHRIST

After this Jesus revealed himself again to the disciples by the Sea of Tiberias, and he revealed himself in this way. (John 21:1)

In the last part of the Gospel of John, we read that Jesus appeared to His disciples after His resurrection. Why was His appearing important? Thomas could not believe without seeing, and Jesus appeared to him. I believe in this we can see the heart of Jesus. He longs to settle every doubt that comes up in your mind!

Thomas answered him, "My Lord and my God!" Jesus said to him, "Have you believed because you have seen me? Blessed are those who have not seen and yet have believed." Now Jesus did many other signs in the presence of the disciples, which are not written in this book; but these are written so that you may believe that Jesus is the Christ, the Son of God, and that by believing you may have life in his name. (John 20:29-31)

Jesus did not leave Thomas in his doubt and unbelief; He saw what it would take to free Thomas from these chains. The disciples had spent a lot of time with their teacher, and Jesus knew they needed confidence in His resurrection.

He knew in order for them to experience Pentecost they needed an unshakable faith in the reality of His resurrection power. Out of this confidence came a boldness, to the point of giving their lives to the gospel without reservation and fear.

Have we met Christ in this way? We like to quote the verse, "Blessed are those who have not seen and yet believe," but this is no excuse not to have a real encounter with Christ. I'm not saying there has to be a physical encounter, but if we want to be as bold and effective as the apostles, we do need to experience Him in a way that settles all unbelief and doubt. The resurrection of Jesus has to be real, or we will never walk in divine understanding of who He is.

Christ can overcome any doubt. Unbelief has no power in His presence. Thomas said, "I will not believe unless I see," and even though he was a doubter, Jesus said, "I will do it anyway!" Our Lord knows that we, like His disciples, cannot walk in power without a revelation of who He is, He understands all of this.

Seek Him with your whole heart and He will reveal himself to you. He will shatter every doubt, every unbelief, and will bring you out and prepare you for Pentecost.

81 A STABLE SOUL

But let him ask in faith, with no doubting, for the one who doubts is like a wave of the sea that is driven and tossed by the wind. For that person must not suppose that he will receive anything from the Lord; he is a double-minded man, unstable in all his ways. (James 1:6-8)

We have many opportunities in life to become anxious and worried. Our enemy tries to use our mind to bring chaos into our lives. The more we begin to understand his attacks on our thought life, the more we can take every thought captive to make it obedient to Christ.

The Bible warns about being "double-minded." What is double-minded? Isn't a double mind one that rests in Christ one minute but slides into doubt and anxiety as soon as life throws a curve ball? Anxiety results in our becoming people who are controlled and manipulated by our feelings. Feelings can never be trusted; a man who allows his life to be guided by his emotions is a man who will be tossed like a ship on a raging sea.

There is nothing stable in man himself. The Bible says for "all flesh is like grass and all its glory is like the flower of grass. The grass withers, and the flower falls…:" (1 Peter 1:24). Today it is here, tomorrow it is gone! How brittle and unstable our lives, if all we have is what we can come up with ourselves. How helpless and hopeless, when we think we can make life happen on our own.

What, then, is single-mindedness? The man who lives in single-mindedness is the one who has found a steady anchor for his soul. That steady anchor is the Word of God. Outside circumstances will never be stable, but His Word endures forever.

> *"But the word of the Lord remains forever." And this word is the good news that was preached to you. (1 Peter 1:25)*

> *"Heaven and earth will pass away, but my words will not pass away." (Matthew 24:35)*

Faith in His Word is the most brilliant invention! Our heavenly Father saw how much this would do for mankind. He saw how much man needed this for stability and security. He saw how little man had on his own and He wanted us to come to a place where we recognize our need for His intervention in our lives. Faith connects us and gives us an anchor for the soul.

The old hymn "It is Well With my Soul" has inspired many. Horatio Gates Spafford, who wrote the lyrics, lost his four daughters when the ship they were on sank. He came to a place where he understood he could have stability in his soul even after a great loss, and he penned the words, "Whatever my lot, Thou hast taught me to say, It is well, it is well with my soul."

Life can be brittle and unpredictable, but there is One who has the power to bring stability into every facet of our life. This can only come through applying His Word directly to our everyday circumstances. Learning how to do this is a process, but once we've learned, we become single-minded, and our soul finds rest like never before.

82 THE POTENTIAL OF A SEED

He put another parable before them, saying, "The kingdom of heaven is like a grain of mustard seed that a man took and sowed in his field. It is the smallest of all seeds, but when it has grown it is larger than all the garden plants and becomes a tree, so that the birds of the air come and make nests in its branches." (Matthew 13:31-32)

This is one of my favorite Bible verses. It shows how much potential is in the seed of the Word of God. The small seed can look like nothing, but it ends up becoming the largest plant in the garden.

The smallest choices in life can lead to the greatest success in the eyes of God. Choices that we think don't matter—and maybe we could get away with doing the opposite and no one would ever notice—may be just such a seed. A man who takes shortcuts will find himself in a place of regret. A seed that is planted will eventually grow up to be a plant, good or bad. The seeds we sow most in life will end up being the greatest part of our harvest tomorrow.

The power of sowing seeds in silence is detected by few, but the man who has learned this truth has learned integrity. Those of integrity know that God is watching when no one else is. The man who does not walk by this truth will one day discover a disaster. It is foolish to think a man can hide his coming harvest. What a man does in silence will one day become an open book for all to read.

83 DEAD TO SIN

What shall we say then? Are we to continue in sin that grace may abound? By no means! How can we who died to sin still live in it? Do you not know that all of us who have been baptized into Christ Jesus were baptized into his death? We were buried therefore with him by baptism into death, in order that, just as Christ was raised from the dead by the glory of the Father, we too might walk in newness of life. (Romans 6:1-4)

Baptism into Christ is a powerful thing once we understand the true meaning of it. Sin loses its grip, and a door into resurrection power opens up, even as we walk on a sin-cursed earth.

Have you ever tried to connect with the world on a carnal level and you walk away and say to yourself, "I simply can't connect"? And then you find yourself trying again, only to repeat the same words. "I simply can't connect!" It becomes pointless. You have nothing in common. Everything seems strange and lifeless.

Once we understand that we have lost our connection to sin, sin becomes useless, good for nothing.

This is what baptism is to those who have been baptized into Christ. Our desire for sin dies, and the name of Christ becomes the center of our focus. We now draw our life from the Word of God. Our appetite drastically changes and everything in life takes on a brand-new meaning.

These all died in faith, not having received the things promised, but having seen them and greeted them from afar, and having acknowledged that they were strangers and exiles on the earth. (Hebrews 11:13)

You might feel like a stranger here on this earth at times, but most likely if this earthly system feels strange, you can bet that you will feel at home in Heaven. The Kingdom of Heaven has a value system that is much different from the kingdom of this world. You should not be able to connect here!

The good news is the Kingdom of God will be established here on earth at a certain time. The cry of our hearts always needs to be, "May Your Kingdom come, may Your will be done on earth as it is in Heaven!" Until this is established, the saints will never feel at home on the earth.

May the Lord give us direction, that we would not waste our time trying to connect with sin when we've been baptized into Christ. May we understand His Kingdom is not of this world. May Christ be our focus, and may we live in the newness He has brought us into through rebirth.

84 LEAVE IT TO THE REAPERS

There are times we look at situations and ask, "Should I do something about this? Try to set things right?" This can be a tough one. I believe we need to hear from God on each specific situation, but Jesus gave us this parable to think about:

He put another parable before them, saying, "The kingdom of heaven may be compared to a man who sowed good seed in his field, but while his men were sleeping, his enemy came and sowed weeds among the wheat and went away."

"He said to them, 'An enemy has done this.' So the servants said to him, 'Then do you want us to go and gather them?' But he said, 'No, lest in gathering the weeds you root up the wheat along with them. Let both grow together until the harvest, and at harvest time, I will tell the reapers, "Gather the weeds first and bind them in bundles to be burned, but gather the wheat into my barn."'" (Matthew 13:24-25, 28-30)

Harvest time might not be tomorrow or next week, but there is a day of harvest coming, and you can trust in this reality. We look at the condition of the world and we look at the condition of the church, and we ask if God will send reapers to go out and take care of the weeds right away. God says the reapers will gather the weeds when harvest time is here. God is in control and we must give Him control.

Our duty is a duty of prayer. Praying for those around us, for hearts to be turned to the Lord. Asking God to give us direction in all areas of our lives so that we respond out of wisdom, having discernment from God about difficult situations.

I believe a man who can give a situation to God, stepping away from it and allowing God to deal with it, will experience the hand of God on this situation in a powerful way. Our best choice is to forgive those who have violated us, blessing them instead of cursing!

If you have gotten the wrong hand of the deal, take courage, child of God. The Bible says the hairs of your head are numbered. If He numbers even the hairs of your head, don't think for a moment that injustice will not be made right. The question is: Do you trust God to make the wrongs right?

Any time someone is pushing, know that this will not always be this way. God sees through all the motives and intentions of a man's heart, and He cannot leave this alone forever.

85 A HEART OF FAITH

For people who speak thus make it clear that they are seeking a homeland. If they had been thinking of that land from which they had gone out, they would have had opportunity to return. But as it is, they desire a better country, that is, a heavenly one. Therefore God is not ashamed to be called their God, for he has prepared for them a city. (Hebrews 11:14-16)

Can a man have faith without having his eyes and heart on a kingdom that is not of this world? Only when we truly desire a better, heavenly country and we have set our heart only on His Kingdom can we operate in the fullness of faith and trust. Faith that comes from a deep-seated trust and surrender to our Maker cannot be overcome by hell itself.

The man of self desires to be in charge and control his own life rather than trusting in his Maker. But the one who learns faith comes to understand that his will must be completely laid down in order to walk in divine faith. We have a habit of thinking faith produces ease, and we fail to understand that a foundation of faith is not easily established unless the old self man is dead.

What did the life of Jesus look like from age 1 to 30? There is little recorded about His life until His ministry starts, but the Bible does say, "Although he was a son, he learned obedience through what he suffered" (Hebrews 5:8). Makes me wonder sometimes how difficult His life was. I tend to think His path was anything but ease. Would we have been tempted to also question whether this could possibly be the Son of God?

And then we read of John the Baptist, who was born a few months before Jesus and grew up to be a voice crying in the wilderness. Such a life does not sound appealing to us in our day. Not sure we could find any volunteers for this. This is how John spent his life, until his voice could not be tolerated any longer by those who lived in sin's luxury.

Those who lived in obedience to faith learned how to stand and discovered a foundation that could not be shaken. Their heart was set on seeking God's Kingdom.

In Hebrews chapter 11 we read of many who walked by faith. By faith Noah. By faith Abraham. By faith Enoch. By faith Abel. By faith Sarah. By faith Moses. Gideon, Barack, Samson, Joseph, David, and Samuel and many more prophets. Could my name be in this chapter of faith? Could I say *By faith,* _____ and add my name and whatever I have been called to? We must learn to walk by faith. We might not be there yet, but we must be heading in the direction of faith, trust, and confidence in our Ceator that cannot be shaken.

- - - - -

When we seek our own comforts more than we seek Him, we prove to God that we don't trust Him. We think we know better; we think we don't need Him. Our blindness keeps us from seeing how much more help is available to us, and we choose the little strength that we have in ourselves. Why not walk in His strength and spend more time in His presence, when His offer is to fight our battles?

Do we believe He will fight for us, or do we find ourselves in the trap of relying on our own strength, exhausted, wondering why the world seems to be prevailing against us?

> *And Moses said to the people, "Fear not, stand firm, and see the salvation of the LORD, which he will work for you today. For the Egyptians whom you see today, you shall never see again. The LORD will fight for you, and you have only to be silent."*
> *(Exodus 14:13-14)*

Faith is confidence that the Lord will fight on our behalf. Nothing in life is more valuable and worth more than confidence in our Lord.

86 A DESERT PLACE APART

The ministry of Jesus was well established and He knew who He was; however, it was a hard time for Him when He heard the news that John the Baptist had been killed in prison.

When Jesus heard of it, he departed thence by ship into a desert place apart: and when the people had heard thereof, they followed him on foot out of the cities. (Matthew 14:13 KJV)

No matter your success in life, there will always be times when you need to find a remote place away from the all the noise and connect with your heavenly Father. In those quiet moments before the day starts, we can pour out our hearts before our Father in Heaven. Jesus found this place of strength, the source of His power. He knew his Father in Heaven; He knew the source of His strength. His mission field was people, but His battles were fought in a place apart, alone with His Father.

The people followed Him, and He ministered to them, feeding the 5000. Then, He sent the disciples across the lake in a boat, and

After he had dismissed the crowds, he went up on the mountain by himself to pray. When evening came, he was there alone. (Matthew 14:22-23)

Jesus understood His need for time alone and He knew His source of strength was to be found when no one else was around. Is this why the disciples asked Him to teach them to pray? They saw that whatever He was doing was extremely effective.

And after six days Jesus took with him Peter and James, and John his brother, and led them up a high mountain by themselves. And he was transfigured before them, and his face shone like the sun, and his clothes became white as light. And behold, there appeared to them Moses and Elijah, talking with him. (Matthew 17:1-3)

What an opportunity! This was one time when these three disciples could go with Jesus to His time of prayer. They experienced for themselves what He experienced on the mountain. I believe they needed this. Jesus wanted them to experience His connection with His Father, and He took them with Him to the Mount of Transfiguration.

The time to establish a relationship with the Source of our strength is not when calamity strikes. The difference between the five wise virgins and the five foolish virgins illustrates this. The five wise bought oil in the good times; they did not wait till times of desperation. The foolish virgins did not see their need in the good times. One of the biggest mistakes a person can make is not seeking God in good times, because every person will come to a place in life where they need a breakthrough.

In today's world, every man is after success, but few are willing to pay the price for true eternal success. Few see how desperately they need time in His presence. Few forsake their own desires for the desires of their heavenly Father. Few have learned to pour out their heart in a place apart, a place where all distractions are forsaken, a place of forsaking their own strength and exchanging it for the strength that comes from Heaven.

Understanding our need for a relationship with our heavenly Father is vital. Only in this relationship can we walk in the place where we are called to walk. Only when we see our desperate need will we find access to a higher place. The greatest guarantee to find this is time spent alone with the Father, as Jesus did.

87 THE POWER OF TRUST

But those who trust in the LORD will renew their strength; they will soar on wings like eagles; they will run and not become weary, they will walk and not faint. (Isaiah 40:31 CSB)

For the Scripture says, "Everyone who believes in him will not be put to shame." (Romans 10:11)

Trust in the LORD with all your heart, and do not lean on your own understanding. In all your ways acknowledge him, and he will make straight your paths. (Proverbs 3:5-6)

Cast your burden on the LORD, and he will sustain you; he will never permit the righteous to be moved. (Psalm 55:22)

The LORD is my strength and my shield; in him my heart trusts, and I am helped; my heart exults, and with my song I give thanks to him. (Psalm 28:7)

Commit your way to the LORD; trust in him, and he will act. (Psalm 37:5)

Honor the LORD with your wealth and with the firstfruits of all your produce; then your barns will be filled with plenty, and your vats will be bursting with wine. (Proverbs 3:9-10)

The Bible has so much to say about trusting in the Lord. Our enemy is out to try to destroy our trust in our Creator.

The serpent came to Eve in the garden with the goal of planting a seed of distrust in Eve's mind. This opened the door for disobedience and brought a separation between Adam and Eve and their Creator. If only Eve would have looked at the snake and said, "I choose to trust my Creator!" Imagine the difference of outcome.

It is no different today. The enemy comes to God's people, wanting them to question whether God has good intentions for them or not. Our enemy wants us to fight for ourselves rather than trusting in our God.

A wise man finds confidence in his God, but the foolish man has no confidence in the Lord's ability. The Lord knows if you trust Him, and only in trusting is His supernatural power released in your life.

REVELATION: ONE NUGGET AT A TIME

The foolish man has learned to fight for himself, but the confidence of the righteous is in the Lord's ability. The wicked fights for himself, but the righteous man has learned surrender. The man who is not able to trust in the Lord has no place of rest.

How can we show the Lord that we have put our trust in Him? One way is by giving God our firstfruits. Doing this, we tell Him we trust Him. Learn to trust God, and it will reward you many times.

Life is a battle of trust: we will either trust in the Lord, or we will trust in the strength of our own hand. Only when we trust in the Lord will He fight for us in ways we can never imagine. So

> *The man who is not able to trust in the Lord has no place of rest.*

when God puts His finger on something in your life, don't resist. This could be the thing that sets you free beyond your wildest imagination.

88 JESUS' RESPONSE TO HYPOCRISY

Then Jesus said to the crowds and to his disciples, "The scribes and the Pharisees sit on Moses' seat, so do and observe whatever they tell you, but not the works they do. For they preach, but do not practice. They tie up heavy burdens, hard to bear, and lay them on people's shoulders, but they themselves are not willing to move them with their finger. They do all their deeds to be seen by others." (Matthew 23:1-5)

Jesus had little patience for the scribes and Pharisees when he saw the hypocrisy and pretense consuming them. They were so concerned about cleaning the outside of the cup (Matthew 23:25), but inside they were full of dead men's bones (v. 27).

We can look at the scribes and Pharisees and ask how they could not see the truth. But unless we are a follower of Christ and see our lives as crucified with Him, our heart looks no different than theirs. Man's natural instinct is to attempt to look good, no matter what's inside. God looks at this in the opposite way; He is more concerned about the inside than He is about the outside.

It would have been one thing for them not to enter into the Kingdom of Heaven, but they wanted to keep others from entering in as well (Matthew 23:13). Whenever there is hypocrisy and wrong motives, man is often threatened by those who want to do what is right.

They offered up service to God but forgot about justice, mercy, and faithfulness (v.23). Perhaps the most dangerous thing they did was reject the people God sent to help them. They killed the prophets that were sent by God (Matthew 23:37).

One of the great things about living in this country is our freedom of speech, and whenever we don't agree with someone, we have been taught and are encouraged to voice our opinion. This can be good and bad. As Christians, we don't always need to voice our thoughts on every issue. Oftentimes, this is rejecting people that God has brought into your life to help you. They might rub you the wrong way, but I believe God is more concerned about how you respond to conflict than He is about you sharing your opinion.

Wisdom knows when to speak and when to shut up! There are times to communicate your opinion and times when silence is the way to kill conflict. Proverbs 17:28 says even a fool appears to be wise when he keeps his mouth shut. When emotions are stirred and the flesh wants to manifest itself, consider wisdom. Once a word has left your mouth, you cannot bring it back. You can find forgiveness, but there might still be consequences.

There is much freedom found in the fact that mankind can put his life in the hands of his Creator, knowing that He is a God of justice, mercy and faithfulness. Trusting in who He is will put your soul to rest and bring you to a place of confidence in Him.

89 A GENEROUS SOUL

One gives freely, yet grows all the richer; another withholds what he should give, and only suffers want. Whoever brings blessing will be enriched, and one who waters will himself be watered. The people curse him who holds back grain, but a blessing is on the head of him who sells it. (Proverbs 11:24-26)

The blessing is poured out on the generous soul. Whenever God pours oil into a vessel, there needs to be a way to get the oil inside; if you don't have a place where God can pour oil in, this indicates that there is also no outlet for you to pour out into other people's lives. The same spout that receives oil needs to be the same spout where the oil flows back out.

The Bible says that it's more blessed to give than to receive. If all we do in life is receive, then we will always have barely enough to make it through. But once we come to a place where we have more than enough and we can pour out into other people's lives, we find this is where the true blessing is. God does not fill you only so you have enough for yourself; there is always a higher purpose than self. God has every intention in life to use you once you are filled, but we can stop the flow whenever our eyes are on ourselves.

Maybe today you find yourself in a place where you feel you can't give much, but every person starts somewhere. If we do not learn to give what we have, giving will never be a real part of our life.

The enemy of our soul wants us to fall into condemnation whenever we feel like we can't give. The solution is coming to a place where we can receive and be filled in order for us to be a blessing in other people's lives. We see the perfect example in the life of Jesus. The Bible indicates that Jesus often went to a place of prayer to commune with His heavenly Father. He knew that if He wanted to give, He needed to be filled.

A generous soul cannot help but give because this person has learned the highest blessing in life is to be able to give what we have in order to receive more fresh oil. The one who always thinks they cannot give will be a person who ends up being empty at the end, with no oil for himself.

Whoever sows sparingly will also reap sparingly, and whoever sows bountifully will also reap bountifully. Each one must give as he has decided in his heart, not reluctantly or under compulsion, for God loves a cheerful giver. And God is able to make all grace abound to you, so that having all sufficiency in all things at all times, you may abound in every good work. (2 Corinthians 9:6-8)

Oftentimes the problem is that we are still fighting for ourselves rather than trusting God. Once the heart trusts in God, a person will be giving with a cheerful heart because they have found the heavenly Father to be a Father of grace and all sufficiency.

God does not want you to give unwillingly, under force. God loves a cheerful giver. The condition of your giving will determine the condition of your receiving.

Whoever brings blessing
will be enriched,
and one who waters
will himself be watered.
Proverbs 11:25

---

90 A REVELATION OF WISDOM

Again I saw that under the sun the race is not to the swift, nor the battle to the strong, nor bread to the wise, nor riches to the intelligent, nor favor to those with knowledge, but time and chance happen to them all. (Ecclesiastes 9:11)

King Solomon, writer of the Proverbs, understood that time and chance happen to us all. If you receive this revelation, it will change everything in your life.

One of the main tactics of our enemy is to convince us that we can never be like others who walk in what appears to be success. He tries to put blocks in your mind, so that you think you are not good enough, you're left out, a "drag behind."

But the Holy Spirit is here to convince us that time and chance happens to all. If you can hear what He is saying, many chains will break from your life. Once the Holy Spirit sheds light on the enemy's lie, you will begin to see that it's not about how good you can be, but rather how good your God is. And He gives time and chance to all.

Solomon walked in a revelation of wisdom. The Lord blessed him with wisdom, and he used it to guide the people. He had a way of inspiring people to follow him and understood what people needed in life. And he had a way of getting this wisdom from the Source of wisdom. Today we have the Holy Spirit. If only we could comprehend how much wisdom and knowledge is laid up for us in the Kingdom of God!

> *"And the LORD will make you the head and not the tail, and you shall only go up and not down, if you obey the commandments of the LORD your God, which I command you today, being careful to do them, and if you do not turn aside from any of the words that I command you today, to the right hand or to the left, to go after other gods to serve them." (Deuteronomy 28:13-14)*

The Lord's desire is to make you the head and not the tail. That you would no longer be a "drag behind" but one who knows how to stand for truth. Out of this He will promote your life! If we take the time we have and allow Him to shed His revelation of wisdom on our lives, our lives will dramatically change.

91 WHO WILL YOU CONFESS IN THE SPOTLIGHT?

In this world we see the rise and fall of kings; one comes in and another goes out. I believe God puts people in positions and God takes people out of positions. Maybe we should ask ourselves the question: If I were put on stage and the spotlight would be on my life, whose name would I draw attention to?

At that moment, one of the most powerful things a man can do is to confess in public the name of Jesus Christ. Is there anything else that matters more than us lifting His name when we have the opportunity to choose whose name gets lifted high?

One might ask what the big deal is of confessing His name in public. Don't forget what the Word says about whoever confesses Him before man.

> *"And I tell you, everyone who acknowledges me before men, the Son of Man also will acknowledge before the angels of God, but the one who denies me before men will be denied before the angels of God." (Luke 12:8-9)*

It is not a light matter as to whether or not we are willing to confess Christ before man—no matter if we are in the position of king or servant. Confessing the name of Christ and lifting up His name brings a new meaning and purpose to our lives.

The man who lives his life under the heavy conviction that the name of Christ must be confessed in public is the man who walks in the fear of God. And the Bible says that the fear of the Lord is the beginning of wisdom. The man who walks in this wisdom and fear of God will not say, "I will confess his name tomorrow" when he has an opportunity today! Tomorrow is never promised.

"So teach us to number our days, that we may apply our hearts unto wisdom," wrote the psalmist (Psalm 90:12 KJV). Part of wisdom is knowing our days are numbered and walking in that knowledge, using whatever time we have to lift His name above all else.

Our time on earth is a gift, and what we do with what time we have becomes vital. If we see that time is a gift, we will be careful not to squander it. Only a fool fritters away his time and does not consider that his days are numbered.

Never waste an opportunity to confess the name of Christ; never underestimate the power of a simple confession. Our words might seem so insignificant now, but His words will be so important to us when we hear Him confess our name before the angels of heaven!

92 PASSION FOR RESURRECTION

I tell you this, brothers: flesh and blood cannot inherit the kingdom of God, nor does the perishable inherit the imperishable. Behold! I tell you a mystery. We shall not all sleep, but we shall all be changed, in a moment, in the twinkling of an eye, at the last trumpet. For the trumpet will sound, and the dead will be raised imperishable, and we shall be changed. For this perishable body must put on the imperishable, and this mortal body must put on immortality. When the perishable puts on the imperishable, and the mortal puts on immortality, then shall come to pass the saying that is written: "Death is swallowed up in victory." (1 Corinthians 15:50-54)

How easy to get wrapped up with the mortal side of life, forgetting that our primary goal is not here and this life is only a taste of eternity and our immortal life. The best time a man experiences on earth is only a feeble spark of the glory awaiting those who love God, those who find their heart leaping whenever they hear the name of Christ proclaimed.

The apostle Paul wrote,

But whatever gain I had, I counted as loss for the sake of Christ. Indeed, I count everything as loss because of the surpassing worth of knowing Christ Jesus my Lord. That I may know him and the power of his resurrection, and may share his sufferings, becoming like him in his death, that by any means possible I may attain the resurrection from the dead. (Philippians 3:7, 10)

Every individual must ask himself the question: Is knowing Christ the center of my heart's desire?

Henceforth there is laid out for me the crown of righteousness, which the Lord, the righteous judge, will reward to me on that day, and not only to me but also to all who have loved his appearing. (2 Timothy 4:8)

Do you long for His appearing? The more we walk in an awareness of who He is and what He is asking of us, the more we fall in love with Him and our utmost desire is for His return. When we long for His appearing, we have the confidence that we will not be strangers to Him when He comes for us.

So today use every opportunity you have to confess His name, knowing that there's a resurrection coming for all mankind.

93 REJOICE, O BARREN ONE

Do you find yourself trapped in a barren land where everything around you and inside you seems dried up? The fruitfulness you once dreamed of seems gone, with no hope of it coming back? Throughout the Word of God, we read of those who had lost hope finding a place of rejoicing.

For it is written, "Rejoice, O barren who does not bear; break forth and cry aloud, you who are not in labor! For the children of the desolate one will be more than those of the one who has a husband." (Galatians 4:27)

In Paul's letter to the Galatians, he reminds us that in a barren place, the Holy Spirit sees an opportunity to bring back the thing that looks hopeless with no chance of resurrection. There are many examples of this in the Word, but by far the best one is Jesus, dying and buried. Then the power of the Holy Spirit showed up!

The desolate place is not a bad place to be if we understand who the Holy Spirit is. It is a place where we know our own abilities do not reach and in ourselves there is nothing that is going to be enough.

Jesus' natural mind was so attacked that He cried out to His Father, "Why have you forsaken me?" In the natural, it was over, all life was gone. He found Himself in a desolate place, with no chance of coming back. But there was another power at work—the Holy Spirit was not lacking anything! Jesus gave up His life as a seed planted, and the power of the Spirit grew a harvest of salvation.

When your resources come to an end and there is nothing you could naturally do to escape the pit you find yourself in, don't forget—this is where resurrection begins! This is where He brings strength when all your strength is gone! This is where joy comes in and rejoicing begins! This is the beginning not the end!

Rejoice, O barren one. As a child of God, you have been birthed into His family. There is a plan for your life, regardless of the desolate pit you might find yourself in today.

Weeping may tarry for the night, but joy comes with the morning. (Psalm 30:5)

94 SEEKING WHOSE APPROVAL?

For am I now seeking the approval of man, or of God? Or am I trying to please man? If I were trying to please man, I would not be a servant of Christ. For I would have you know, brothers, that the gospel that was preached by me is not man's gospel. For I did not receive it from any man, nor was I taught it, but I received it through a revelation of Jesus Christ. (Galatians 1:10-12)

A revelation of Jesus Christ is not given to us through a fellow man but rather the person of the Holy Spirit revealing Christ in our hearts. Only when we understand this do we walk in a reverence for God rather than trying to please those around us. Whoever we are trying to please is the one we are a servant to.

The one who understands that pleasing God is to be first in their life will not be comfortable with the things promoted by this world. For example, the world glorifies man's ability to fight for himself, whether that means taking advantage of his fellow man or simply honoring natural strength above the strength that comes from the Holy Spirit.

We can become distracted so easily from our main purpose in life and find ourselves trying to please people, but is there anything of more value than understanding and having a personal relationship with Christ? Our ultimate focus in life needs to be to walk in a greater revelation and depth of salvation. The blood that was shed for our souls need never be wasted. The greatest mistake a fool makes is to neglect so great a salvation by trying to please his fellow man.

How is salvation neglected? Mostly by having our eyes and attention on something outside of Christ. Our attention can so easily be drawn away from Christ and our desires rest elsewhere rather than on our Savior.

One thing that gauges who has our attention is how much time we spend in the Word of God. Having time in the Word first thing in the morning before the day starts will dramatically change the way a person lives the day. Whoever gets our attention first at the beginning of the day will also be the one who tends to influence us during the rest of our day.

The Holy Spirit opens our understanding and causes us to comprehend the revelation of Jesus Christ, but we need to have a desire for Him.

We need to be asking the Holy Spirit to create within us a deep longing to understand the depth of the heart of our Father in Heaven.

One word from the Holy Spirit can so dramatically change a person's life. Just one word! The problem is oftentimes that we do not ask, because we are trying to please someone or something else outside of Christ. But when our eyes are on Him and He has our attention, there is nothing He cannot accomplish.

95 SOWING IN SILENCE

Do not be deceived: God is not mocked, for whatever one sows, that will he also reap. And let us not grow weary of doing good, for in due season we will reap, if we do not give up. So then, as we have opportunity, let us do good to everyone, and especially to those who are of the household of faith. (Galatians 6:7, 9-10)

There are times when we sow in public and times when we sow in silence. Never underestimate the power of sowing in silence. This is where we are tested as to whether or not we trust God with the seed that no man knows we have sown.

There is a God and He sees every move we make; we can rest assured the seed sown in silence will one day become a crop of overflowing abundance.

And without faith it is impossible to please him, for whoever would draw near to God must believe that he exists and that he rewards those who seek him. (Hebrews 11:6)

What a weight falls from our shoulders when we understand we can be transparent and keep sowing seeds of righteousness, regardless of whether seen or unseen in man's eyes! Our struggle, the unnecessary weight we carry, is often that we are influenced by the world's gauge of success. But our Lord and Savior said that His Kingdom is not of this world (John 18:36), and our work is in *His* Kingdom, not that of the world.

Jesus knew His Father, and He knew His mission was to bring salvation to many souls. He knew He would die on a cross and look like a fool, but it was to bring salvation to a lost and dying world. He was willing to sow a seed in a dishonorable way for the salvation of mankind. Today we have been called to have the mind of Christ and to do life the same way He did. Whether we look like a fool to the world or not doesn't matter, as long as His purpose is accomplished in our life.

Your day of reaping is coming. Keep sowing seeds of righteousness and you will look back and marvel at His grace on your life. The time frame is not yours to decide. He will give you a harvest in His time.

96 HYPOCRISY

We do not need to be suspicious people who are always thinking in the negative, but we need to be aware that not every person who smiles is a true friend.

There will be people in your life who are only after information because their heart desires gossip more than anything else. All they want is to seek out your weaknesses in order to turn around and tell someone else who you are. You might ask why this matters. Don't cast your pearls before swine! This is why we need the Holy Spirit's discernment concerning whoever we meet.

How pure is *your* life? How clean are your motives? When someone meets you, do they walk away saying, "I have no doubt; I sense integrity all the way." Can they say, "I know he is not a backstabber. I feel it when I get close to him. I believe it's not in him to hurt anyone"?

Christ is coming back for a pure bride, a bride that has no hypocrisy. One who is without guile.

> *And in their mouth was found no guile, for they are without fault before the throne of God. (Revelations 14:5 KJV)*

The dictionary's definition of *guile* is *deceitful cunning.* The fool might ask, "What is wrong with guile?" Today's world teaches people to be cunning, sneaky, and deceitful and then turns around and calls this wisdom. Does your sneaky and deceitful take away from those who are innocent? Does your cunning make sure that you are taken care of first? Only you can answer these questions.

Jesus never considered guile an option. I believe this is why the scribes and Pharisees could not handle Jesus—His motives were so pure it made them uncomfortable. Their hypocrisy had no way of hiding. When He was on trial and asked about His teaching, He said, "'I have spoken openly to the world. I have always taught in synagogues and in the temple, where all the Jews come together. I have said nothing in secret'" (John 18:20).

It's always our full duty to give our best to whoever comes into our life, regardless of what we get in return. The only thing that we should never do is cast our pearls before swine. There's no way you can get this right without being led by the Holy Spirit. Love all people, but be wise who you choose for your closest friends.

97 A FOLLOWER OF CHRIST

Understand this, my fellow man: When our eyes are on Christ, our feet will follow.

We cannot have our eyes on the world and expect our feet to follow Christ. Whenever my eyes find Christ, my feet will follow. The problem is that many times we begin looking at things outside of our Master, putting those things at the center of our focus, and then we wonder why there's no passion to follow Christ.

Whenever you get thrown into a difficult situation, do yourself a favor and ask the Holy Spirit to take your eyes where He wants your feet to go. Recently I found myself in such a situation, and I felt the Holy Spirit impress on my heart to ask Him to take my eyes where He wanted my feet to follow. I believe this is often how He leads people where they need to go. The Bible tells us to run our race "looking unto Jesus, the author and finisher of our faith" (Hebrews 12:1-2). Again, where our focus is, our feet will follow.

After the resurrection of Jesus Christ, He appeared to his disciples. They needed to see who they were following—a resurrected Christ, not a dead one! The last they had seen of their Teacher was at His crucifixion or as the body was laid in the tomb. But they were not left with that as their focus; He appeared to them so they would have a resurrected Christ to follow.

So today ask yourself the questions, What am I looking at? Am I a follower of Christ? Is my focus on His Kingdom first? Is anything more important to me than keeping my eyes on Him?

When our eyes are on Christ,
our feet will follow.

98 THE BLOOD OF JESUS

In him we have redemption through his blood, the forgiveness of our trespasses, according to the riches of his grace.
(Ephesians 1:7)

Has your heart been cleansed by the blood of Jesus? Has your mind been renewed by the power of His Word? He reaches and draws out those in the lowest pit and sets them up for a display of His powerful glory!

He looks at the lowest sinner and says, "One drop of My blood applied will make you almost unrecognizable to those who have known you in your old life. Today, all things have become new. My blood cleanses, and the power of My Word will renew your mind."

How lost and how low the old sinner used to live, but today he can say, "I've been cleansed by the blood of Jesus. My life has never been the same. Glory has filled my soul, and today I live only by the power of the gospel. Now the Holy Spirit has space to work in my life however He desires."

Oh, the power of having a life that is fully given to the Trinity! The power of no longer being in charge of your own life! There is so much potential in the power of the Holy Spirit in our lives—if only we can give our lives to Him without reservation and keep from being distracted.

Do you understand the glory that waits for those who have given everything to their Master? Do you understand the glory that waits to fill your soul even as you walk on a sin-cursed earth? Do you understand the power that fills a man's soul when the Holy Spirit takes over?

All the power and all the glory became ours when our Savior gave His life and shed His blood for the redemption of mankind. Child of God, never underestimate the power that is released because the life of Jesus Christ was given for mankind.

We get glimpses of His glory while walking here on this earth, but nothing will compare to the moment when we see our Savior face-to-face!

99 ANXIOUS FOR NOTHING

Do not be anxious about anything, but in everything by prayer and supplication with thanksgiving let your requests be made known to God. And the peace of God, which surpasses all understanding, will guard your hearts and your minds in Christ Jesus. (Philippians 4:6-7)

Not that I am speaking of being in need, for I have learned in whatever situation I am to be content. I know how to be brought low, and I know how to abound. In any and every circumstance, I have learned the secret of facing plenty and hunger, abundance and need. I can do all things through him who strengthens me. (Philippians 4:6-7, 11-13)

How quickly the peace of God leaves a soul when anxiety comes in! But Paul said he had learned how to face plenty, hunger, abundance, and need. He went through beatings and was left as dead more than once. He was on a ship when they found themselves in a natural disaster. He learned how to be okay regardless of circumstances. He learned how to say, "It is well with my soul." He understood his God never changed, regardless of what was going on around him. He understood what happened to him could never cause him to lose his salvation because he was grounded in Christ.

Life will never be easy. If you're looking for a life of ease, you will be disappointed. Those who find the peace of God are those who have learned God's peace is available regardless of circumstances and God's peace can flood the soul in the midst of turbulence.

There is an anchor for your soul in the midst of trouble. No one might know the depth of your turbulence, and no one might know the things that are coming against you, but there is One you can trust. He has witnessed everything possible to mankind, whether it is peace or the lack thereof. Learn to trust in your God, because seasons come and seasons go, and when the storm has passed through, His steadfastness will mark you and set you apart.

The more mature we become in our faith, the more we understand that the trying of our faith produces steadfastness. A powerful verse in the book of James tells us,

> *For you know that the testing of your faith produces steadfastness. And let steadfastness have its full effect, that you may be perfect and complete, lacking in nothing.*
> *(James 1:3-4)*

"Perfect and complete, and lacking in nothing" comes from a life of steadfastness. And steadfastness is learned under trial. Those who have walked in faith have come to understand that under a trial, a man has the potential to become the express image and likeness of Christ.

If Jesus the Son had to learn obedience through the things He suffered, are we any better? Steadfastness only comes through the trying of our faith. The next time a circumstance in your life brings pressure, understand that He wants to produce in you a stability that will set you apart from those who have no confidence in their God.

> *And my God will supply every need of yours according to his riches in glory in Christ Jesus… The grace of the Lord Jesus Christ be with your spirit. (Philippians 4:19, 23)*

100 THE DEFENSE OF THE GOSPEL

Have you ever wondered what your purpose is in life? Paul said he was put here for the defense of the gospel.

> *Some indeed preach Christ from envy and rivalry, but others from good will. The latter do it out of love, knowing that I am put here for the defense of the gospel.*

What then? Only that in every way, whether in pretense or in truth, Christ is proclaimed, and in that I rejoice. (Philippians 1:15-16, 18)

Our heart should beat for the defense of the gospel. Maybe you're not 100 percent sure what you're here for, but I believe we have been called to stand for the gospel in all its fullness. What an honor to be given the role of defending the gospel of Jesus Christ! There will be those who think we're fanatics, or think we take life too seriously. Remember, the early church gave their physical lives for the gospel, and if we could ask them today, I'm sure none of them would regret the life they surrendered to Christ.

What a joy that we have an opportunity to stand for the One who died for us! What a joy to understand the calling placed on one's life! When we walk in this place, standing for His name, confessing Him in public, the Word says He will confess us before the angels of heaven.

A man who has learned to stand for Christ in public, confessing freely the name of Jesus, is a man who knows what it is to walk in true freedom. We have been called to liberty, to stand for the name of Jesus Christ without apology. Many people who don't have the courage to confess Christ in public would love to do so if only their pride were not controlling their life. We have been called to be a light in the darkness. We can't waste our time!

101 REMEMBER, HE SAVED YOU!

But God, being rich in mercy, because of the great love with which he loved us, even when we were dead in our trespasses, made us alive together with Christ... For by grace you have been saved through faith. And this is not your own doing; it is the gift of God, not a result of works, so that no one may boast. (Ephesians 2:4-5, 8-9)

Remember, He is the one who saved you and He is the one who will keep you saved. But how easily we forget!

We begin in His mercy and grace, and we continue in His mercy and grace. If the Holy Spirit would leave us, we would be lost in a short amount of time. We have no right to be saved outside of Christ. We might have natural giftings and talents that man praises, but when it comes to salvation, we must put honor where honor is due.

In Galatians 3 we read some strong words from Paul to the church:

> *Let me ask you only this: Did you receive the Spirit by works of the law or by hearing with faith? Are you so foolish? Having begun by the Spirit, are you now being perfected by the flesh? (Galatians 3:2-3)*

We begin our walk with Christ in faith, and then how easily we are tempted to think that our own piety somehow keeps us saved! Look to Christ, our only true Source.

102 THE LAND OF BLESSING

> *Now the LORD said to Abram, "Go from your country and your kindred and your father's house to the land that I will show you. And I will make of you a great nation, and I will bless you and make your name great, so that you will be a blessing." (Genesis 12:1-2)*

Is there a land that the Lord would love to show you but you are still clinging to things from your country, kindred, or father's house? I believe a true blessing cannot come without learning to let go.

Whenever God does something extraordinary, He asks the person He is using to exchange what they have for something from above. And often to the natural man this will not make any sense. If it would make sense, there would be no cross involved; but it is only when a man embraces the cross and learns to give what he has back to his Maker that true blessing is released!

Our natural man has learned to grab and hold on instead of letting go and allowing God to do what He wants to do. Hebrews 4:15 says Jesus was "in all points tempted as we are." I believe even He had to learn obedience in this letting go. If He had not, would He have been able to endure the cross, to go through with His assignment that brought us life?

Don't think for a moment that it was easy for Abram to leave his country, his kindred, and his father's house. And don't think for a moment that after he had finally received the promised son Isaac, it was easy for him to offer back to God the promise that had come from God.

In most of the biblical stories, we only read of what is accomplished, rather than understanding what people needed to go through to get them there. If the size of their testing was as dramatic as the size of their accomplishments, one's heart could almost burst at the thought of the amount of pressure they must have been under. Those who have been through the fire understand that God's promises often come after the heat has been turned up, the test has been passed, and they learn to believe God.

Abraham became the father of many nations.
Noah saved his household through the flood.
Paul wrote much of the New Testament.
Joseph saved his family in the drought.
Moses led the children of Israel out of Egypt.
Elijah killed 450 false prophets.
Isaiah the prophet prophesied about the promised Messiah.
David killed Goliath and was anointed king.
John the Baptist baptized the promised Messiah.
Jesus became the Savior of the world.

And the list goes on and on.

What we see are these accomplishments, but it would do us much good to go back and understand the process that got each man to this place. I believe if we could see the path that needs to be traveled for such accomplishments, most of us would likely never choose it.

If you find yourself on a path of much difficulty, ask the Lord to use you wherever He desires. He can use the person who is broken, surrendered, and believing God's Word when facing much testing. But the person who is brittle and cannot go through a trial will never see his life become useful in a powerful way.

> *When we give our difficulty to our Master, He uses it to make us into what He desires.*

Only when we give our Master right-of-way in our life are we guaranteed to be made into His likeness. Only then will true light come bursting forth from our life in a powerful way.

103 A BAPTISM INTO CHRIST

We live in a time when words seem to be so cheap. A person might make a commitment, but if they don't get perfect results, it's easy to make an excuse and opt out of and cancel that commitment. It's so easy to bail out on people. Commitment and relationships have little value. The biggest problem with this mindset is that nothing is sure.

When Jesus' followers committed to follow Him and were baptized in His name, there was no turning back. They committed to Him, knowing it would likely cost their physical lives. Often in today's world, we like to pride ourselves in the fact that we prayed the sinner's prayer—but commitment has never been fully established by many. If, when you committed to Christ, you knew that it would likely cost you your physical life, would you do it?

This is why baptism in the name of Christ was such a powerful thing for His followers. They were marked in public and not ashamed to die for Christ. Whenever and wherever the gospel came in, there was much conflict with the works of darkness. The gospel was a sword that divided light from darkness, a force that would divide sheep from goats, righteousness from unrighteousness. And those who wanted to hide their sin became uncomfortable. Jesus' followers knew this.

Those who were in a desperate situation and needed a change in their lives rejoiced to see the day when the Messiah finally made His appearing. But those who thought they could do life on their own, not knowing how empty and lost they were, had no need for Him and wanted to have Him crucified.

If only we could convince the world today to make a clear distinction between light and darkness, righteousness and unrighteousness, pure and impure, committed and uncommitted. If only we could bring back the power of baptism into Christ, in which we make a commitment and stand on it with desperation, knowing that it will cost everything we have. Today, it seems like we have watered down commitment to Christ to the point where it's hard to tell the difference between Christianity and the world's self-help programs.

Is this why Jesus asked the question, "When I come back, will I find faith on earth?" (See Luke 18:8) Maybe He meant, "Will I find this kind of commitment? Will I find a people who are committed when they are baptized into My name? Will I find a desperate cry that does not stop until they find the reason why they were born?"

Jesus made this statement right after He was talking about the persistent widow, who did not stop seeking the answer that she needed. Many times, we don't see the desperation of our situation, and for this reason we quit just short of our miraculous breakthrough. Or perhaps we think we can "make it" without an answer, and so we don't find what we need. We settle for less than the miraculous. But in this parable, the widow did not stop until she got the thing she needed.

When the Son of Man comes, will He find faith?

104 EMBRACING PAIN AND DIFFICULTY

How easy it is to spend our entire life trying to get away from difficulty and pain. Our culture has taught us that our goal must be ease.

When Jesus taught His first disciples, I believe they understood that a person can be full of the joy of the Lord in the midst of difficulty and pressure. They knew if they took a stand for the gospel, they would face extreme opposition. But they also understood that this released the joy of the Holy Spirit in their lives. The only way to have true joy was to welcome the Word of God, knowing difficulty was a part of it.

> *The joy of the Lord can only be experienced when we embrace the path He has for us.*

Physical birth does not come without discomfort. We know that, and yet we would like to think that in our lives here on earth we can have new birth and growth without difficulty or pain. We all like the idea of God birthing a time of new growth and moving forward in our life, but many cannot embrace what comes with growth. If we want to avoid pain, we'll avoid birth. But once we learn we *need* to embrace difficulty and pain, birth becomes a guarantee.

Our sights need to be set on the will of God above anything else life puts in our path. When the fear of God fills a person's life and the will of God becomes his goal, then he can forget about obstacles being a hindrance and he can navigate his way to success.

Paul understood that his life had been given to his Master, whether it meant living for Christ or dying for Christ.

> *I eagerly expect and hope that I will in no way be ashamed, but will have sufficient courage so that now as always Christ will be exalted in my body, whether by life or by death.*
> *(Philippians 1:20 NIV)*

He was not afraid to face whatever pain was pointed at him because he understood life was far more than comfort. He understood what it was to be sold out for Christ. No amount of pain and suffering could change who he was committed to. His conversion was real. His commitment was written. There was no going back. He considered his life spent for Christ.

Today, we must ask ourselves a question: What problems am I avoiding, and what mindset is keeping me from fulfilling His perfect will for my life?

The joy of the Lord can only be experienced when we embrace the path He has for us. This is where we find true vitality and strength. The joy of the Lord is your strength. Don't let pain and difficulty discourage you from embracing the joy!

105 ARE YOU AN OPEN BOOK?

Adam and Eve were the first to try to hide what they had done, and that has been the tendency of mankind ever since—to see what he can get away with, thinking no man will ever notice. But the Bible tells us if a man lives to be a hundred and hides his sin all the way to his grave, the moment he slips into eternity everything is revealed and there are no more secrets.

> *The sins of some people are conspicuous, going before them to judgment, but the sins of others appear later. So also good works are conspicuous, and even those that are not cannot remain hidden. (1 Timothy 5:24-25)*

Wherever Jesus went, He was an open book. He hid nothing. The scribes and Pharisees hated Him for this. They wanted to keep things covered, but He was here to do the exact opposite. In the place He came from, there are no secrets regarding the sin of man!

Some sins are conspicuous. The definition of *conspicuous* is "standing out, so as to be clearly visible." Some people's sins are obvious, seen during their lifetime. Others are hidden. But even though some people's sin seems to stay covered for now, this is never a long-term reality.

When something is coming against me as an individual, it's easy to ask God to uncover it. But what about the things I find myself caught in that might be hurting someone else? Understanding that nothing that is hidden will stay hidden brings me to a place where I become an open book and have no use for anything related to a hidden agenda or hypocrisy.

As Christians, we have been called to walk a path where the light of the gospel has the right-of-way to shine on any wrong motive or hidden agenda for self-gain. There is no individual who will not be held responsible for their own motives and actions. As we grow up into Christ, we come to a place where we understand hiding sin is completely useless.

And no creature is hidden from his sight, but all are naked and exposed to the eyes of him to whom we must give account. (Hebrews 4:13)

One day there will be no secrets. Everything that is hidden will be brought out in the open for all to see. The sooner we come to a place where we understand this truth, the better off we are. We might as well hide nothing.

106 IS MONEY GOOD OR BAD?

For the love of money is a root of all sorts of evil, and some by longing for it have strayed from the faith and pierced themselves with many griefs. (1 Timothy 6:10 NASB)

But those who crave the wealth of this world slip into spiritual snares. They become trapped by the troubles that come through their foolish and harmful desires, driven by greed and drowning in their own sinful pleasures. And they take others down with them into their corruption and eventual destruction. Loving money is a root of all evils. Some people run after it so much that they have given up their faith. Craving more money pushes them away from the faith into error, compounding misery in their lives! (1 Timothy 6:9-10 TPT)

"But seek first the kingdom of God and his righteousness, and all these things will be added to you." (Matthew 6:33)

And God is able to bless you abundantly, so that in all things at all times, having all that you need, you'll abound in every good work. As it is written: "They have freely scattered their gifts to the poor; their righteousness endures forever." (2 Corinthians 9:8-9 NIV)

As for the rich in this present age, charge them not to be haughty, nor to set their hopes on the uncertainty of riches, but on God, who richly provides us with everything to enjoy. They are to do good, to be rich in good works, to be generous and ready to share, thus storing up treasures for themselves as a good foundation for the future, so that they may take hold of that which is truly life. (1 Timothy 6:17-19)

In this, we could have many questions, and who is able to answer them all?

Does God want His people to overflow with blessings of material gain? Or would He rather see a person live a life where finances are always a struggle?

I believe God wants to pour out His blessing on every person even more than we can imagine. But His ultimate concern is that our heart desires a connection with Him more than we desire anything else; that our heart would find strength in His presence first; that out of this strength, He would be able to bless His people so much they cannot contain it; and that the overflow would be so great that many others could also be blessed. Let us never get wrapped up with a one-sided focus on the blessing rather than the One from whom all blessings flow.

Is it that so many have found the blessing, but not the One who blesses? The God who blesses is the one who wants a relationship with His people. His people were never designed to find blessing and not the Blesser. We can spend our entire life chasing after success and never find the true Source. What a tragedy to find the flow of blessing and never find the One who gave it!

Man has been placed on a planet where he has needs along with desires to find true purpose and meaning in life. One thing for sure is that the man who seeks Christ with undivided attention will find answers that most are not willing to pay for.

No true satisfaction for the soul is found apart from seeking our Creator first, above all things.

Finding a place of faith in God is the most valuable thing a person could ever find. Faith should never be forsaken for anything other in life, because when we lose confidence in our Creator, our lives begin to deteriorate.

How can a man know whether or not he is seeking God's Kingdom first? Can a man know when his desire is God more than anything else? Can a man know when his motives have been purified and all self has been burned out and forsaken? Whether or not a man knows his own state is debatable, but I believe our Creator has no problem with seeing into the heart of man and knowing why he does what he does. To our Creator, everything is open and exposed. And part of the work of the Holy Spirit is to guide us into truth about these very questions.

So today if you have breath, use it to glorify your Master in Heaven. Use it to seek His Kingdom first. Desire a land that is beyond the natural, and watch what God will do. Let him use you however He desires, and He will make sure your life is loaded with His blessing, *whatever* you need to abound in His work.

107 UNDERSTANDING

As for what was sown on good soil, this is the one who hears the word and understands it. He indeed bears fruit and yields, in one case a hundredfold, in another sixty, and in another thirty. (Matthew 13:23)

Wisdom is the principal thing; Therefore get wisdom. And in all your getting, get understanding. (Proverbs 4:9 NKJV)

The definition of *understanding:* to perceive the meaning of; grasp the idea of; comprehend; to be thoroughly familiar with; apprehend clearly the character, nature, or subtleties of.

As we can see in the parable of the sower, the one who understands, or comprehends and grasps the meaning of the Word, will be the one who bears fruit. Proverbs says that in all our getting, we must get understanding, If comprehending and understanding is so vital for the Christian, how can we be guaranteed to get it?

Another key to this is given in Jesus' words in Matthew 6:33: "Seek ye first the kingdom of God, and all these things shall be added unto you." It is when we stop having double vision, when we seek His Kingdom with a single focus and purpose, that we find the understanding we are looking for. I believe God gives us desires so that He can guide our lives where He knows we need to go; and when we yield to these desires or inspirations, He moves us into deeper understanding.

Oftentimes, we do not believe that we can simply come to the Lord and ask for wisdom and understanding—and that He will then give it. But once we believe He is our Father and He listens when we ask, the limitations are taken off and we enter into a place of comprehending the goodness of God. We must believe that He is and that He is a rewarder of them that diligently seek Him.

It has nothing to do with our goodness, but it has everything to do with our believing in the goodness of our God. His goodness is available to us if only we pause and look to Him for all our answers in life. Our enemy's goal is to distract us and cause our eyes to see double vision; but once we focus on Him alone, we will see an overflow of His presence in our lives.

Give me understanding and I will obey your instructions; I will put them into practice with all my heart. (Psalm 119:34 NLT)

108 SOLOMON AND JESUS

At Gibeon the LORD appeared to Solomon in a dream by night, and God said, "Ask what I shall give You." And Solomon said... "Give your servant therefore an understanding mind to govern your people, that I may discern between good and evil."
(1 Kings 3:5, 6, 9)

What if we encountered God in a conversation such as this? What is it that we would ask for?

Solomon wanted wisdom for the benefit of God's people. He knew he needed an understanding mind, discerning good from evil. His desire was to rule the people well and help them live according to God's instruction.

When we have a decision to make that will either help people or help ourselves, which would we choose? Jesus followed a path He knew would help mankind but would lead to His own death, all while He Himself did not have a place to lay His head. All He cared about was that He would manifest our Father in Heaven to a lost and dying world.

The disciples understood the benefit of giving their lives for their Teacher, especially after Jesus was raised from the dead. They saw firsthand what a life of giving without holding back looks like.

Followers of Christ, we also have to make the choice: give our lives to help others or focus on our own needs.

In taking an opportunity to help humanity, we at times also take the risk of being misunderstood. Are we okay with being misunderstood and maybe suffering for doing right?

Suffering for doing wrong is expected, but what about suffering for doing what is right? Is there enough of Christ manifested in our life that we have the endurance and patience to suffer for doing right?

Two men were crucified with Jesus. One understood that what he was suffering was a consequence of his lifestyle, but the other one never acknowledged that; he was still willing to lay blame elsewhere. And between them was the Savior, who had lived a perfect life without sin, and still ended up being crucified, dying for the sins not only of those two but of the whole world.

The perfect way to suffer is for doing right, but the next best is allowing your suffering to lead you to Christ as did the one thief on the cross. The worst way to suffer is for your own wrongdoing and never recognize your own consequences.

So today, when you get a chance to suffer for doing right, don't waste this opportunity to glorify your Savior, who did this thing well.

109 PURIFYING REDEMPTION

[The Lord declares] "For I will be merciful toward their iniquities, and I will remember their sins no more."
(Hebrews 8:12)

Has it become real to you that Jesus Christ paid the price for you to be free from all generational iniquities and sins?

What is an iniquity? The dictionary defines it as wickedness, sin, and injustice.

When we miss the mark and end up bringing hurt to those we love or to our own lives, it is easy to make excuses and say, "That's my natural tendency." Or we can face it and say, "This is *iniquity*."

He entered once for all into the holy places, not by means of the blood of goats and calves but by means of his own blood, thus securing an eternal redemption.

How much more will the blood of Christ, who through the eternal Spirit offered himself without blemish to God, purify our conscience from dead works to serve the living God. (Hebrews 9:12, 14)

He paid for our complete redemption! There is nothing that He has not accomplished for us. Let us not forget the price He paid to cleanse us from all unrighteousness.

110 EATING THE BREAD OF LIFE

So Jesus said to them, "Truly, truly, I say to you, unless you eat the flesh of the Son of Man and drink his blood, you have no life in you. Whoever feeds on my flesh and drinks my blood has eternal life, and I will raise him up on the last day. For my flesh is true food, and my blood is true drink. Whoever feeds on my flesh and drinks my blood abides in me, and I in him. This is the bread that came down from heaven... Whoever feeds on this bread will live forever." Jesus said these things in the synagogue, as he taught at Capernaum. When many of his disciples heard it, they said, "This is a hard saying; who can listen to it?" And he said, "This is why I told you that no one can come to me unless it is granted him by the Father." (John 6:53-56, 58-60, 65)

"Unless you eat the flesh of the Son of Man and drink His blood you have no life in you!" (John 6:53). We, like the disciples, say this is a difficult teaching. What is Jesus saying here?

Somehow, we have fallen into thinking that our desire for God is something we come up with. Unless we have been in a God-forsaken place, we do not understand how little our own ambition has to do with our destination. How easily we forget that everything is a gift of grace. The air we breathe is a gift. Salvation is a gift. All our desires and abilities and ambitions are gifts from above, and at any moment our Creator has the right to pull them from us.

The LIFE in us is a gift.

Have you come to a place where you recognize how empty and useless your life is unless you find the purpose for which you have been born? The Lord knows how to bring a person to this place. It is only in partaking of the life of Christ that we could ever be washed from our sin and saved from hell.

"Eating and drinking the body and blood of Christ" pours the life of God into a person and creates the image of Christ. It is the Spirit who gives life; the flesh profits nothing (John 6:63). Christ magnified and Christ glorified in us by the Spirit is the only way we find Life.

Many were offended when Jesus made this statement, and those who think they are capable of doing life on their own still to this day think these words are foolish. But those who gain understanding learn that there is no life outside of Christ's life in us. He alone is the Bread of Life!

111 BY FAITH

Oftentimes when we hear about walking in faith, we think about supernatural provision and victory. Those are definitely a real part of living by faith, but I find it interesting that Hebrews 11, the chapter of faith, starts with a list of those who walked in faith, found supernatural provision, and conquered; but then the writer switches in the latter part of the chapter and tells us that sometimes faith can be choosing to suffer rather than receiving instant provision, and sometimes it takes difficulty to bring us to a place of reward.

And who are we to say how soon this reward comes?

The opening verses give account of the faith of Abel, Enoch, Noah, Abraham, Sarah, Isaac, Jacob, Joseph, Moses, even the harlot Rahab. Verses 32-35:

And what more shall I say? For time would fail me to tell of Gideon, Barak, Samson, Jephthah, of David and Samuel and the prophets— who through faith conquered kingdoms, enforced justice, obtained promises, stopped the mouths of lions, quenched the power of fire, escaped the edge of the sword, were made strong out of weakness, became mighty in war, put foreign armies to flight. Women received back their dead by resurrection.

Victories! That's what we most often think of when we think of walking by faith. But right here, in the middle of verse 35, the writer makes the switch:

> *Some were tortured, refusing to accept release, so that they might rise again to a better life. Others suffered mocking and flogging, and even chains and imprisonment. They were stoned, they were sawn in two, they were killed with the sword. They went about in skins of sheep and goats, destitute, afflicted, mistreated—of whom the world was not worthy—wandering about in deserts and mountains, and in dens and caves of the earth.*
> *(Hebrews 11:35-38)*

Victory does not always look like victory when it starts out. That's why I believe the Scripture that talks about the Kingdom of God being the least of all seeds. The choices we make can look foolish at the beginning, but the right choices will lead to a life of victory. Popular preference is the instant reward. But the time for our total victory and reward is not up to us to decide.

Sometimes the choices you make will look foolish in the moment, yet those who stand for His righteousness regardless of cost, will end up being a display for the glory of God.

Faith
is trusting God regardless of popular opinion.
Faith
learns to stay usable when circumstances want to
harden our heart.
Faith
will not allow the deceitfulness of sin to corrupt
our confidence in God.
Faith
refuses to take from someone else for self-gain.
Faith
often chooses to take the lowest position to give
room for the glory of God.
Faith
is able to keep its mouth shut when opportunity
arises to glorify self.
Faith
is able to act for the good of others above its own.
Faith
has confidence all wrong things will be made right.
Faith
is trust in God.

---

112 A CLOSER LOOK AT THE HEART OF MAN

The heart is deceitful above all things,
  and desperately sick;
  who can understand it?
"I the LORD search the heart
  and test the mind,
to give every man according to his ways,
  according to the fruit of his deeds."
Like the partridge that gathers a brood that she did not hatch,
  so is he who gets riches but not by justice;
in the midst of his days they will leave him,
  and at his end he will be a fool. (Jeremiah 17:9-11)

How easily man can justify his sin in his own eyes when it looks like the only option he has. He has bought into the lie that in order to make it in life he needs to walk unjustly so that he will not be taken advantage of.

How scary the thought, that man can justify anything to himself! There is no sin that cannot be justified in the mind of man, regardless of how evil it is. The devil is a master at convincing the sinner that his self-help acts are needed to function in life.

The Holy Spirit's presence in our lives is our only chance of ever seeing how evil our sin really is. Only His conviction brings a man to a place where he confesses his sin and is no longer willing to justify it. When we commit a sin and the Spirit's presence overwhelms us, sin can then be dealt with.

When we find ourselves in a place where sin no longer looks like sin, we need to ask ourselves if the Spirit is still welcome in our life. When He is no longer welcome, one of the first things that leaves us is conviction of sin.

The Holy Spirit knows whether or not He is welcome. We are able to fool others and even ourselves, but not so with the Holy Spirit.

He longs to be a part of your everyday life! So today, welcome His presence to be your guide. He will never leave you or forsake you. Pay attention when He brings conviction of sin. Let Him release His promises in His way and His time. Set your heart to be faithful, no matter the cost. Your life will be rewarded.

Every way of a man is right in his own eyes, but the LORD weighs the heart. (Proverbs 21:2)

113 PROTECTED BY ANOINTING

I write these things to you about those who are trying to deceive you. But the anointing that you received from him abides in you, and you have no need that anyone should teach you. But as his anointing teaches you about everything, and is true, and is no lie—just as it has taught you, abide in him. (1 John 2:26-27)

Christ is our anointing. A key to understanding this is understanding how to value His work in our hearts. Having a single eye and desiring Him above all else must be the first step in recognizing the work of Christ in yourself and others.

Your life has been made right through the person Jesus Christ, and this is the anointing that is needed to find a place of rest and contentment. Without Christ in the center of our soul, we find ourselves in a place of restlessness, not understanding the path that God has for us.

As a born-again child of God, never underestimate the power of Christ as a seed in your life. Christ in us and us abiding in Christ. Our enemy longs to bring all kinds of distractions into our lives, but we must never forget the power of Christ living in us. Unless a person is anointed by the person of Christ, there is no chance to find true purpose in life.

It is Christ's presence that gives man guidance outside of himself. Man no longer needs to do life guided by his own senses, but now a Helper has been sent. Unless we learn to depend on the person of the Holy Spirit, we cannot be guided effectively.

The question is: Do those who come in contact with us walk away thinking, "I have seen Christ today?" It's easy to show people our natural gifts, but it's more important that people see Christ in us. Have we learned to step aside and allow Christ to come forth? The Holy Spirit longs to reveal Christ to others, and he needs men and women who think more of Christ than themselves.

Learning to hear His voice and refusing to be distracted is the test that faces God's people. Today, your only true protection is Christ in you and allowing the Holy Spirit to do what He desires.

114 SEEING HIM AS HE IS

Beloved, we are God's children now, and what we will be has not yet appeared; but we know that when he appears we shall be like him, because we shall see him as he is. And everyone who thus hopes in him purifies himself as he is pure.

No one who abides in him keeps on sinning; no one who keeps on sinning has either seen him or known him.

No one born of God makes a practice of sinning, for God's seed abides in him; and he cannot keep on sinning, because he has been born of God. (1 John 3:2-3,6, 9)

To be like Christ, we must see Him as He is and abide in Him. It is when we abide in Him, where sin has no right to live, and His seed abides in us, that we are changed and nothing in our life stays the same.

All the self-help programs in the world have no chance of changing the heart of man. It is only when we comprehend who Christ is that chains fall from our hearts and the personality and character of Christ become a real part of our lives.

How can we understand and comprehend the character and personality of Christ? This can only be revealed to us by the Holy Spirit Himself. And we must desire this thing above everything else life has to offer.

A great danger in the church today is that we will come to a place of not desperately needing a revelation of Jesus Christ. He was not received by those who didn't need Him, but was sent to those who knew that without Him, they wouldn't make it!

I believe the level of our need for our Savior will determine the depth of our revelation of who He is. When a person makes the decision that their most important goal in life is to know Christ, the Holy Spirit is given the right-of-way to bring the revelation of Jesus Christ into their life.

One of the enemy's strongest tactics against Christians today is to bring distractions and passions that take God's people away from desiring Christ. When a man no longer desires Christ, the battle seems lost. Even though many good things do come through our modern lifestyle, one of our biggest cautions must be against this strategy of distraction and wrong passions.

The person who keeps his focus on Christ can overcome his enemy, because the seed of Christ remains in him. Our prayers today need to be that we keep Christ at the center of our focus, because only in this will there be overcoming power poured out by the Holy Spirit. We must keep our eyes on Him—and in this, watch what God will do!

The seed of Christ in our hearts is the anointing needed in our lives. Abiding in Him keeps our eyes on Him. Only in this will we find power to overcome the enemy, as the Holy Spirit takes us from glory to glory and to a deeper revelation and understanding of the Father, Jesus Christ, and Holy Spirit.

115 THE PATH CALLED LIFE

The heart of man plans his way, but the LORD establishes his steps. (Proverbs 16:9)

Come now, you who say, "Today or tomorrow we will go into such and such a town and spend a year there and trade and make a profit"— yet you do not know what tomorrow will bring. What is your life? For you are a mist that appears for a little time and then vanishes. Instead you ought to say, "If the Lord wills, we will live and do this or that." As it is, you boast in your arrogance. All such boasting is evil. (James 4:13-16)

How easy it is for us to slip into thinking we are in charge of our own lives, forgetting that every breath we take is a gift from above. How easy it is for us to think our life consists of only the years we have and the temporary things we possess and accomplish here.

We so easily settle for a carnal reward that will vanish in a moment, never to be seen again. We become narrow minded and forget about eternal investments. In the natural, we are convinced of the importance of long-term earthly investments—but what about eternal investments? The only thing that matters in this earthly life is the seeds you sow that will grow fruit for eternity. To be faithful in your sowing will bring a harvest that you could never plan for, so if you get a chance today to sow a seed, remember the potential for the next life.

Herein lies the problem: The natural man cannot see beyond the realm he lives in. He gets so attached to the things he can touch, taste, and see, that he cannot imagine living life without them.

But the man who is born from above sees this natural realm is only a dim shadow of things to come and things that cannot be seen. It takes the spiritual man to recognize that time spent on earth is a preparation for heavenly glory that goes way beyond anything the natural mind could comprehend.

This is why Jesus could go to the cross, despising the shame of it. He understood there was a life above the natural. More than the natural. Better than the natural. Way beyond the natural!

It is only revelation that takes us beyond the natural realm and lets us see as He saw, giving us insight into a realm that is far from this natural one,

---

If you get a chance to sow a seed,
remember the potential
for the next life.

---

116 DIFFICULTIES AND JOY

As we read accounts in the Bible, we see how much difficulty those who went before us had to endure. However, it seems like the more difficulty laid out before them, the more chance that person had to decide to walk in the joy of the Lord. The more difficult circumstances we face, the more opportunities we have to choose the joy of the Lord.

Difficult situations have never kept our Master from bringing His presence into a person's life as an overwhelming joy of the Lord. In fact, it seems He hardly ever does this unless a person is under pressure.

Out of the seven churches to whom Christ gave messages through John's Revelation, only the church in Smyrna did not get a rebuke. This church was facing tremendous tribulation and poverty, but Christ also emphasized that they were rich!

"And to the angel of the church in Smyrna write: 'The words of the first and the last, who died and came to life. "'I know your tribulation and your poverty (but you are rich) and the slander

of those who say that they are Jews and are not, but are a synagogue of Satan. Do not fear what you are about to suffer. Behold, the devil is about to throw some of you into prison, that you may be tested, and for ten days you will have tribulation. Be faithful unto death, and I will give you the crown of life. He who has an ear, let him hear what the Spirit says to the churches. The one who conquers will not be hurt by the second death.'"
(Revelation 2:8-11)

To the natural mind, this should never be—that God calls them rich, even though they were in the midst of tribulation, facing poverty, and about to be martyred for the name of Christ! God's definition of "poverty" and "empty" is completely opposite from the way man thinks. "Empty" is to be without Christ, and "poor" is to not know the One who died for you.

If we want to be rich in life, salvation is the only thing that guarantees abundance. Tribulation will force us to see this reality. Tribulation will make us take a closer look at what is true value in the eyes of God and cause us to choose joy that comes when everything around us looks grim and wasted.

> *Difficulty could not keep the Holy Spirit*
> *from bringing Jesus out of the grave,*
> *and difficulty will never keep*
> *the Holy Spirit from entering your*
> *situation, penetrating the darkest grave*
> *you might find yourself in.*

When we discover true salvation that brings joy to our inner being, outside circumstances have no control over our life. The man who wrote a great part of the New Testament was a man who spent a lot of time writing in a prison cell, with his hands and feet in chains. Yet his heart found joy in the midst of all his circumstances. Today we read his letters and our soul finds the words as food and life, but we tend to forget the crushing that he went through to see the depth of true life.

So today when you find your life being crushed and you wonder why, let the difficulties do the work in you that needs to be done, so that you can be a fountain in a dry desert for others who need answers in life.

117 WHY THE GREAT TRIBULATION?

Why would God allow mankind to face a tribulation so intense that many people won't be able to endure the pressure? It will be so much so, that the atheist will stand back and say this proves there is not a God.

Then again, why does God allow a woman to have birth pains to the point she wonders, "Will I survive this?" But after the child is born, she rejoices in the fact that new life has come!

The problem is that oftentimes we become so narrow-minded we forget there's a bigger picture and God has something in mind. He tells us, "'When these things begin to take place, straighten up and raise your heads, because your redemption is drawing near'" (Luke 21:28). The carnal man can only see here and now, but God wants us to see the bigger picture.

If we put our eyes where they need to be, we will be of those who find themselves dressed in robes washed white in the blood of the Lamb, where condemnation cannot touch us and we are known for a pure conscience. Our eyes must be on the bigger picture or we will be caught off guard. We must see tribulation as birth pains for a better plan from our Creator. He has redemption in mind, and He knows tribulation will open up mankind to receive the fullness of who He is. It will force humanity to see life from His perspective.

Jesus could have asked the same questions: "Why should I drink this cup? Why the wilderness, to be tempted by the devil? Why do I have to learn obedience through the things I suffer? Why do I have to be hated by many who seek my life? Why do I get accused for doing a good deed on the Sabbath?" He knew His heart was pure and He had yet many things to suffer, but He knew it was for a greater plan. He knew there was a bigger picture. He counted His life as nothing in order for a higher plan to be fulfilled.

So when you see tribulation in the future, rejoice! There's a bigger plan. These are called birth pains, and the day is coming when all will come together and make perfect sense. Our Creator would never allow tribulation for tribulation's sake. He is our master, and He has His eyes on a plan so amazing that one day all you will say is "Holy, holy, holy! Glory to the Lamb, who was willing to redeem mankind to lead us to a place where perfect peace once again reigns this earth as God's original intent!"

118 WALKING IN THE REVELATION OF CHRIST

And their eyes were opened , and they recognized him… They said to each other, "Did not our hearts burn within us while he talked to us on the road, while he opened to us the Scriptures?" (Luke 24:31-32)

The most devastating condition of a person's life is when a spiritual blindness overtakes them and keeps them from recognizing Jesus Christ and understanding the reality of our Savior.

We can stand back and point our fingers at those who are not living as Christians, but how often do we fail to recognize our Lord in our midst? How often have we failed to recognize where His work is being done?

When our hearts become hardened, our minds also are darkened and we do not grasp the reality of who He is. We may think we carry a little more light than the person beside us, but that does not say we're walking in the revelation of Christ as was intended by our Father in Heaven.

No man's life can stay the same when he believes in Jesus Christ and when the Holy Spirit is real to him. Only when we believe the Holy Spirit is with us can we then walk in a place of true meaning and understanding.

Why could the people around Jesus not accept Him as Messiah? I believe it was because they had an idea stuck in their minds of who and what He should be. Maybe their hearts had been hardened by difficulties, and they were not open to anything different from what had been deeply ingrained in their minds. How easy to let the things that come against us destroy our ability to receive the reality of Christ and the Holy Spirit.

If we do not learn obedience through our trials, our hearts can become hardened by suffering. The Bible says Jesus learned obedience through the things He suffered. And yet, we see many people in today's world become hardened by difficulties. What makes the difference?

The things we suffer will either lead us to a deeper revelation of Christ or will bring us to a place where we can't be used in His Kingdom. The things that come against us should bring us to our knees, where we put our total confidence in our Father and the Holy Spirit takes over and changes our lives.

How vital to recognize the intent of the Holy Spirit and His plan and purposes for us! How essential to understand that He is with us and will never leave us alone!

The disciples were told to stay in the city until they were clothed with power from on high. This power cannot be real in our lives if we do not recognize Him. Once we do recognize Him and understand He is with us and we are coworkers with Him for the plans of Heaven, then we can receive power from on high.

119 APPROVED BY WHO?

As humans, we have one time slot, one chance to run a race and run it well. One chance to learn how to function in faith and understand who our Father is. One opportunity called Time. And then, what was written will stay written!

The definition of sin is "missing the mark," missing the mark of walking in faith. The snare that entraps many is looking to mankind to hear words of approval instead of recognizing that our approval must come from above. Many desire to hear the words "Well done" only from a fellow man rather than from our Father in Heaven after life has been written.

If we could only hear the thoughts of those who have run their course before us, it would settle so much of our striving. They would tell us there's only one approval that is needed and it does not come from man. They would tell us how flimsy man's approval is when considered against approval or disapproval of our Maker. Our enemy's goal is to blur the lines so that we do not comprehend how important it is to be approved by the One who made us in the beginning.

The fear of man is a snare, making us unable to recognize what truly matters. Pride is a departure from reality. The fear of God is understanding that His approval is the only thing that matters. Humility is understanding that without Him, I can do nothing.

The temptation always stands before us: Whose approval do you want?

> *"His master said to him, 'Well done, good and faithful servant. You have been faithful over a little; I will set you over much. Enter into the joy of your master.'" (Matthew 25:23)*

120 TRUST BEYOND HERE AND NOW

How easy it is for us to take matters into our own hands, refusing to trust our heavenly Father. Our heart may be hardened and we might see no other option but to fight for ourself. Fear may find its way into our soul and trust will sound like a strange thing to do. The natural realm we live in seems to be the only thing that is real, and resurrection sounds like a strange idea.

The truth is, the natural man cannot receive the things of the Spirit. What he can touch, taste, and smell are the senses he lives by every day. But the one who lives by the Spirit understands there is life beyond the natural. The power of the cross helps him see beyond this realm, into a realm that is far more real than here and now.

Why do you think Jesus could endure the cross, "despising the shame for the joy that was set before Him"? Was it not because He believed there was life beyond the grave? Was it not because He knew Someone who could fight for Him beyond the natural? He understood it was foolish to fight for Himself. He understood His strength did not come from Himself.

Struggles in life often come because we fail to see beyond here and now. The man who learns faith and learns to see beyond the natural is the man who puts his confidence and trust in a God who has the power to do beyond anything he could think or imagine.

So today when you come to a place where your strength has been exhausted, know that this is where His strength becomes real and life goes from natural to supernatural.

121 "To You It Has Been Given"

And he answered them, "To you it has been given to know the secrets of the kingdom of heaven, but to them it has not been given. 'For this people's heart has grown dull, and with their ears they can barely hear, and their eyes they have closed, lest they should see with their eyes and hear with their ears and understand with their heart and turn, and I would heal them.' But blessed are your eyes, for they see, and your ears, for they hear. For truly, I say to you, many prophets and righteous people longed to see what you see, and did not see it, and to hear what you hear, and did not hear it." (Matthew 13 :11,15-17)

Our ability to multitask is a gift from our Creator for our lives in the natural realm, but when it comes to our daily devotional life, multitasking should never be considered an option. The person who can focus on the Word of God and shut everything else out is the one who has the ability to go farther in His Kingdom.

In today's world, so many things demand our attention, trying to bring distraction from our real purpose for being birthed and living in a sin-cursed world.

We all face it whenever we sit down for time spent in the Word. We are tempted to have divided attention, our mind wanders, and it's difficult for us to keep our eye single and focused on Christ alone.

If we can only see and reject the distractions that have been set up against us! They are meant to keep us from moving forward into a life of abundant purpose and meaning, where our hearts become saturated with the person of Jesus Christ, the Kingdom of God becomes real, and divine purpose grabs our attention.

Jesus had much to say about this subject. In one place we read His words, "But seek first the Kingdom of God and His righteousness, and all these things shall be added unto you." In order to seek His Kingdom first, we need to give Him undivided attention, without distraction.

Those who have made a difference in the past were those who made up their mind and decided not to be distracted from serving their King. Our heavenly Father can do much when we give Him undivided attention with no restrictions. Then, when we open the Word, it becomes a personal letter and we can see clearly the reason why our Savior gave His life.

Jesus told His disciples, "To you it has been given to know the secrets of the Kingdom of Heaven." What an opportunity! Many desired to know this secret and yet they could not attain it. This is the greatest gift we can ask for: to have the scales taken off our eyes and be able to see and understand clearly the person of Christ.

He is the one who takes the scales from our eyes and causes the mind to comprehend the fullness of who He is. Without this gift from above, we will never comprehend salvation. This is why the early disciples gave their lives for His Kingdom—they understood everything in life was useless outside of knowing the depth of His salvation. When salvation is found in a real way, is it any wonder one would be willing to give his own life for this treasure?

For some, the story of Jesus crucified is only a story in history. For others, the gospel of Jesus Christ affects them deeply and salvation makes its way to their heart and everything changes. When we read the Scriptures, does the Word move us deeply and penetrate every negative emotion, or is it something that we have a hard time comprehending?

He has the power to take the hardness of our hearts and instead saturate our hearts by the reality of who He is. Ask and you will receive, seek and you will find. The one who redeemed us paid the price to bring us the fullness of salvation. Give Him your undivided attention.

122 JESUS MARVELED

"Lord, my servant is lying paralyzed at home, suffering terribly."
And [Jesus] said to him, "I will come and heal him." But the
centurion replied, "Lord, I am not worthy to have you come
under my roof, but only say the word, and my servant will be
healed... When Jesus heard this, he marveled and said to those
who followed him, "Truly, I tell you, with no one in Israel have I
found such faith." (Matthew 8:6-8, 10)

This passage contains some of the most astounding words in the
Gospel of Matthew.

The centurion came to Jesus with a desperate situation. It's easy to
glance over this chapter and forget the suffering that was going on in
this centurion's servant's life. Oftentimes we do not understand the
depth of suffering until it touches our own life or those we love. He
was desperate, and he had an astounding faith that is hard to find in
our world today—and in Jesus' day. Even Jesus marveled at the
centurion's faith.

The centurion was a man of worldly importance, but he knew that
status did not make him worthy for Jesus to even enter his house. He
had seen authority in operation in his own life and in the life of Jesus,
and he recognized that the power of the realm in which Jesus walked
was enough to take care of any situation that needed a touch from the
Creator.

If we could only comprehend the power contained in one word from
Christ, we would save ourselves much heartache and striving. I believe
we often come up with reasons why God would not do the miraculous
for us, and this ends up being a wall that stops us from going where
we need to go. Our thoughts are sometimes what stops or restricts the
work of our Creator. Thoughts that come as unbelief are a barrier,
resisting faith in Him.

[Jesus] said, "Truly, I say to you, unless you turn and become
like children, you will never enter the kingdom of heaven.

Whoever humbles himself like this child is the greatest in the kingdom of heaven." (Matthew 18:3-4)

We must see how little strength we have outside of Christ, and enter into trust like a child. When a child hears a word from his father, the child does not have the ability to think it false but receives it as truth. As adults, we are in danger of having a heart of unbelief that resists our Father's voice, thus stopping His words that would set us free. The simplicity of those words can penetrate the deepest calluses and wounds found in our own hearts.

Have our "religious minds" been trained to "work" our way into salvation? The Bible says our own righteousness is filthy rags, yet we so easily forget this truth and think we somehow gain salvation through personal status because of our works or religious upbringing. The simplicity of the gospel is blocked by our unbelief.

Praise God for work ethic and ability to endure when life gets tough, but this can never be substituted for the childlike simplicity that is needed to enter the Kingdom of Heaven. Makes one wonder how many things we have built up in our minds that are only "good ideas" but end up hindering us from walking in the gospel as fully as did this centurion. Our confidence must be found in His Word. We must be able to turn from our own ideas and trust like a child to enter in life in His Kingdom.

Isn't it true that the greater our agenda and the more ideas of our own we hold onto, the less we allow Christ to simply be who He is?

123 THE LORD, MY REFUGE

Thus says the LORD:
"Cursed is the man who trusts in man
and makes flesh his strength,
whose heart turns away from the LORD.

He is like a shrub in the desert,
  and shall not see any good come.
He shall dwell in the parched places of the wilderness,
  in an uninhabited salt land.
Blessed is the man who trusts in the LORD,
  whose trust is the LORD.
He is like a tree planted by water,
  that sends out its roots by the stream,
and does not fear when heat comes,
  for its leaves remain green,
and is not anxious in the year of drought,
  for it does not cease to bear fruit.
The heart is deceitful above all things,
  and desperately sick;
  who can understand it?
I the LORD search the heart
  and test the mind,
to give every man according to his ways,
  according to the fruit of his deeds." (Jeremiah 17:5-10)

As Christians, we quote Bible verses and claim to put our trust in our God, but in this modern day we live in, it is so easy to put our trust in anything but God. We have an abundance of education, science, doctors, and "experts," and we slip into trusting in the hand of the flesh, only looking for help from above when there's no other option.

God our Father can see clearly whether our dependency is on Him or on the system we live in.

Jesus tells the story of the widow who came to the judge asking for justice against her adversary. Even though the judge refused for a while, her persistent asking showed her unwavering faith and caused Jesus to ask, "When the Son of man comes, will he find faith on earth?"

When Christ comes back, will He find a faith that is persistent, showing our Father that our confidence is truly in Him? A faith that stands committed to our heavenly Father regardless of the outcome?

A faith that is surrendered to His power? A faith that has counted the cost and accepts no other option?

We would all say we want the substance of faith in our lives, but few are solely committed to Christ and convinced there is no other help outside of Him. Few have learned obedience through the things they suffer. Few would give their lives for the faith that the early church died for.

When it comes to salvation and the saving of our spirit and soul, the only option we have is trusting Christ for eternal salvation. This same faith takes us deeper, into a place where salvation becomes everything we live by.

Without faith, we have no other way to show our Master that our confidence has been put in His hands. Faith proves to our Lord that we are committed and confident, trusting Him to be Almighty. Only the Holy Spirit can show us all the areas in our lives where our trust has been in the arm of the flesh; only the Spirit can make us honest enough to admit this, repent, and put our confidence in our God alone.

Today, it is important to ask the Holy Spirit to bring this conviction, so that we do not depend on any source outside of the Trinity.

124 BEYOND THE FLESH

It is a challenge to believe in a realm beyond what we can see, touch, or taste! The carnal man depends on the natural things in life, but the man born of the Spirit believes there is more help in the realm that he can't see with his natural eyes. The Holy Spirit operates in the realm that can't be seen; and if the Holy Spirit is not real to us, we will not operate in this realm.

We have learned to depend on the natural, but we need to graduate beyond our dependency on here-and-now. This is what the Bible talks about when it asks us to go beyond the natural. Beyond the carnal man. Beyond the natural senses. Into a realm where all things become possible because the supernatural controls the natural!

In order for this to happen, we must see ourself as crucified with Christ; we must go beyond our feelings and emotions into the realm of the Spirit, where life is, into a realm where Christ is glorified and the Holy Spirit is given the right to operate in a person's life.

> *Now we have received not the spirit of the world, but the Spirit who is from God, that we might understand the things freely given us by God... The natural person does not accept the things of the Spirit of God, for they are folly to him, and he is not able to understand them because they are spiritually discerned. (1 Corinthians 2:12, 14)*

What a disaster for a man to believe only in what he can see with his natural eyes! May our eyes go beyond the help that comes from man! May the realm of the Holy Spirit be more real to us than the natural people we walk with on the earth!

125 CHRIST FORMED IN YOU

Every day we have opportunities to meet people we've never met before. When we do, is there anything about us as Christians that leaves an impression?

"Christian" means we're to be like Christ. If we are to represent Him to the world, shouldn't people be saying, "There's something different about him"? We are human and we make mistakes, but shouldn't there be an aroma about us that leaves a fragrance of Christ wherever we go?

If we were to live in the day when Jesus walked this earth, how would we view Him? There was nothing ordinary about Him. He made a difference, and the scribes and Pharisees did not like it. Everywhere He went, He met either extreme resistance against Him or people would give their lives for Him because they saw Him as Messiah.

How dare we as Christians—"like Christ"— think that we can blend in and not be seen as different in how we treat people, different in character, and different in values, standing with integrity even when there's a cost?

> *The mystery hidden for ages and generations but now revealed to his saints. To them God chose to make known how great among the Gentiles are the riches of the glory of this mystery, which is Christ in you, the hope of glory. (Colossians 1:26-27)*

> *My little children, for whom I am again in the anguish of childbirth until Christ is formed in you! (Galatians 4:19)*

Those who find the reality of Christ being formed in them and Him living inside every detail of their lives have found a life with brand-new meaning. Paul understood this truth, and he was in anguish to see Christ birthed in those he preached to.

If Christ is formed in us, will it be obvious?

Those who trust Him as their personal Savior will graduate into an eternal reward only because Christ has been formed in them. It will not be our own goodness, but only because our life has been hidden in Christ and Christ is formed in us. It will only be His righteousness perfected in us that gives us the license to enter into eternal reward.

And His righteousness perfected in a saint should be obvious here and now!

126 HIS MERCY, NOT OUR FILTH

How easily we can fall prey to a religion that offers a false righteousness, in which we begin to walk as if we create our right standing with our Creator.

Down through the years, humanity has tried to come up with its own righteousness, but in God's Word we read that it is as filthy rags (Isaiah 64:6). The best man can do looks like garbage to our Creator! How foolish to think we can work our way to salvation, when we are dressed in filth instead of righteousness. Salvation brings us to a place where we confess our sin and understand that we are and have nothing outside of Christ.

Our dependency on Christ and His righteousness is what glorifies Him and the salvation He provided. In one place, Paul speaks about how he lost all things for the sake of Christ; he counted everything as lost in order to know the One who died to save him. The fullness of salvation will enter our lives only when we reach a place where we depend on the work of Christ alone.

False religion would teach us to do the best we can and expect God to accept our works. But the true gospel is this: We cannot in any way attain righteousness, and so Christ Jesus died and paid the price for complete salvation. How desperately we need to see the reality that we will never measure up, but for our Savior and His righteousness! We all have a past and it looks quite grim until we understand it has all been blotted out by a single work of Christ. Forever saved and forever forgiven! The glory is due to His name!

When our focus shifts from ourselves to Him, we begin to seek only what comes from above. We begin to understand how little human effort accomplishes outside of Him. Christ's name glorified, His name exalted, is a result of understanding His work on the cross. This is our only license for eternal salvation.

Learn to depend on Jesus Christ and His finished work on the cross, and your life will reflect who He is and not the garbage in your past.

He saved us, not because of works done by us in righteousness, but according to his own mercy, by the washing of regeneration and renewal of the Holy Spirit, whom he poured out on us richly through Jesus Christ our Savior, so that being justified by his grace we might become heirs according to the hope of eternal life. (Titus 3:5-7)

127 TESTING

When times get difficult, could it be that we are being tested? Could difficulty be a time we go through to test our faith in our Lord?

Don't lose heart in difficulty. Don't lose faith. If we recognize what is happening in a test, we are empowered in the midst of it because we understand its purpose.

God purifies saints through difficulty, but how many people lose faith in the midst of a trial because it looks like everything is going wrong? Today, if you find yourself in a place where it looks like things are falling apart, consider Luke 8:13 and 15:

And the ones [where the seed fell] on the rock are those who, when they hear the word, receive it with joy. But these have no root; they believe for a while, and in time of testing fall away.

As for that [where seed fell] in the good soil, they are those who, hearing the word, hold it fast in an honest and good heart, and bear fruit with patience. (Luke 8:13, 15)

Those with good soil understand that a test is only for a moment and in this their heart is purified and the name of Christ is glorified. Their life ends up bearing much fruit through patience and endurance.

Maybe you are being tested, and all God wants you to do is trust Him, because when you trust Him, He will bring you through. Once we see this reality, we will be able to rejoice in the middle of a test and the mighty hand of God is able to accomplish in our life the purposes of Heaven.

And a reminder: He prepares a table before us in the presence of our enemies (Psalm 23:5). Difficulty and complications have never stopped our Father in Heaven from feeding us and accomplishing His perfect plan in a moment of crisis.

All God wants you to do is trust Him,
because when you trust Him,
He will bring you through.

---

128 HAVE YOU STILL NO FAITH?

In this life, storms come and storms go. As long as we live in a world where the natural dominates, this will always be the way it is.

In Mark 4, we read that while the disciples were convinced they were perishing in the storm at sea, Jesus was asleep in the boat. Jesus never lost confidence in His Father; when everyone else was afraid, He slept. Jesus lived in a chaotic world, but this never kept Him from the peace that came from Heaven. He was here to show His disciples how to stay confident and restful when chaos seemed to reign.

How easy it is to lose our inner calmness when we come into a chaotic situation. Those who mature in Christ learn how to keep peace, regardless of what comes against them. This is not an easy thing to do, but when chaos knocks on our door, the responsibility of every believer is to wake Jesus in our boat if we have found Him asleep.

Jesus woke and spoke to the storm and peace came, but we can almost hear the disappointment in His voice when He looked at the disciples and said, "Why are you so afraid? Have you still no faith?" (Mark 4:40).

Have you still no faith? Why are you afraid? Don't you understand your Master in Heaven will never leave you or forsake you? You're in the middle of a storm, but the storm does not determine how much peace can flood your soul. Things are coming against you, but that does not mean He will not give you what you need. He will prepare a table before you in the presence of your enemies. In the middle of a storm, He will flood your soul with peace.

Christ commands Christians to have faith and peace, regardless of circumstances. It is important that we find a place of strength, a place where Christ dwells in our hearts by faith, a place where we are not depending on the faith of someone else.

> *Jesus turned, and seeing her he said, "Take heart, daughter; your faith has made you well." And instantly the woman was made well. (Matthew 9:22)*

Jesus affirmed the faith of the woman who believed she need only touch the hem of His garment to be made well. He did not say, "I have made you well." He saw her confidence in Him and affirmed *her* faith.

It is vital that as Christians we find our own faith and don't depend on the faith of someone else. Faith will give us the strength to comprehend His Kingdom. Without faith we cannot even begin to please our Father. He longs to see a people who have learned to trust in Him, regardless of circumstances.

> *So that Christ may dwell in your hearts through faith—that you, being rooted and grounded in love, may have strength to comprehend with all the saints what is the breadth and length and height and depth, and to know the love of Christ that surpasses knowledge, that you may be filled with all the fullness of God. (Ephesians 3:17-19)*

129 EVERY THOUGHT

We demolish arguments and every pretension that sets itself up against the knowledge of God, and we take captive every thought to make it obedient to Christ. (2 Corinthians 10:5 NIV)

There are few things that have so much impact on a person's life as the mind. It is the mind that is affected by positive or negative influence.

The mind is like a piece of real estate where two people are desiring access, both seeking to call it their own. In the life of any person, this battle is always going on. Our heavenly Father desires possession of this property, the human soul. There is also the enemy of our soul trying to gain access, but his only intention is to bring destruction.

Isn't it in the mind where our enemy aims his attacks and tries to sink the ship of a believer? This is why the Word tells us to take every thought captive to the obedience of Christ. If we could only see every thought that comes at us in one day and then stand back with clear vision to make a decision as to the source of each thought!

The Bible compares lack of discernment to a condition of the soil. There is the "soil" of one who does not understand the Word, the one who is consumed with the cares of life, the one who gets offended when facing a trial, and the one who bears fruit. Our enemy tries to enter the mind to make us anxious about life, offended when we're tested, or unable to understand when we hear. But when we hear the Word, comprehend it, and receive it, our Creator enters and changes our lives forever.

How powerful the mind, that with it a man is able to block the miraculous power that comes from Heaven, that man is able to resist his Creator! The mind is where unbelief lodges and destroys the purposes for which man was born.

But it is also the mind where the miraculous power of God is released and Heaven gains access to live in a person, frees him to walk in a place of divine purpose, and releases the supernatural.

Consider the faith of a child. The mind of a child does not have the ability to block truth—as we often do as adults. How often does more education and more reasoning gained become a block to releasing the person of Christ and the Holy Spirit in a Christian's life?

A child does not consider doubting. They take the word of their earthly parents and believe it. Today, become small enough to take His Word and believe it, without doubt.

130 So That Evil Has No Claim

And now I have told you before it takes place, so that when it does take place you may believe. I will no longer talk much with you, for the ruler of this world is coming. He has no claim on me, but I do as the Father has commanded me, so that the world may know that I love the Father. (John 14:29-31)

Jesus gave His disciples a heads up to prepare them for what was about to come. He knew what lay ahead. Even though His body was destroyed and His soul was attacked, in silence He would forgive those who killed His body. The prince of this world had no claim on Him.

To this day, our enemy seeks to bring destruction into our lives. Often, he does this by inflicting an inner wounding, and it can be so severe that many never find healing and recovery. Jesus bore all of His wounds for our healing, for our freedom from the power and destruction of all darkness. Yet many find themselves trapped by a wounding that can only be overcome by one thing—the forgiveness of our Father in Heaven.

If we want forgiveness for ourselves then we must walk in forgiveness toward those who have violated us. There is no way we can receive forgiveness for ourselves if we don't have the capacity to forgive those who have done us harm.

To walk in a place where the evil one cannot touch us, we must find freedom from the chains of unforgiveness. Unless we receive the revelation of Christ and understand how He released us from destruction and gave us the power to overcome all darkness, we will be so bound up that we can't function. Our enemy does not care how he can accomplish destruction as long as he destroys relationships and keeps the church from true unity in the Spirit.

After Jesus returned to His Father, the Holy Spirit was sent to bring unity in the body of Christ, but this unity can only come when the Holy Spirit is in operation. The Holy Spirit is a person with a personality, and in order for Him to work, there must be a welcoming of how He thinks. In this, people come together with one goal and one purpose.

It is the Holy Spirit who gives the power of forgiveness, heals relationships, and brings people together for an end-time revival.

131 THE ONE WHO REVEALS

Revelation is not produced by man's own hand. It comes only from a higher power.

> *Therefore I want you to understand that no one speaking in the Spirit of God ever says "Jesus is accursed!" and no one can say "Jesus is Lord" except in the Holy Spirit. (1 Corinthians 12:3)*

> *He said to them, "But who do you say that I am?" Simon Peter replied, "You are the Christ, the Son of the living God." And Jesus answered him, "Blessed are you, Simon Bar-Jonah! For*

flesh and blood has not revealed this to you, but my Father who is in heaven." (Matthew 16:15-17)

Man's best efforts produce only filthy rags and corruption. It is good to have learned a good work ethic and come from a culture that has good moral values, but when it comes to revelation, a work ethic and moral culture is never enough to reveal Christ. It will never produce the revelation that Jesus is Lord over everything. It will not bring a man to the understanding that there is nothing the power of the Holy Spirit cannot change. Man cannot bring himself to the place of expectation and confidence that the natural is subject to the supernatural—only the presence of the Holy Spirit brings this revelation.

Many become frustrated because they believe somehow their own works can produce a revelation that Christ is Lord. Whenever we think it's our own works and our righteousness, we frustrate ourselves and those around us and end up in a natural war instead of walking in faith. The atmosphere around us should tell us who is at work: is this my own effort, is this an atmosphere of expectation and confidence in the Holy Spirit?

Nothing in the world can replace the Spirit's presence, and nothing in the world has the ability to penetrate the heart of man and produce faith like our God can! His presence will produce compassion, and His presence will take the natural fight and turn it into faith produced by love.

We all say we want faith and we want the ability to believe in the supernatural help of the Holy Spirit, but with His presence must come a letting go of our own way, a surrender to His way of thinking. His personality will change how we view people. His work in our lives will cause us to give up our need to control. As long as we try to grasp control of our own life, He is not in control. He will not share His glory.

Jesus knew that it was good for Him to leave so that the Helper could be released. He knew it was time for Him to depart; His work was complete and He saw no reason to stick around. Imagine the damage and the restrictions if Jesus had not seen that His time was up. He knew His chapter was written and now He handed over to the Holy Spirit what was meant to be the work of the Holy Spirit. In this there is a vital lesson: When God tells you to pull your hands away from a certain situation, act wisely and listen to what He's saying! Oftentimes, we can't take our hands off and the work of God is stopped because we want to be in control and can't release and let go.

Understand your calling and stay with it. No more. No less. He is the Spirit of revelation and direction, and only when we yield to Him can He produce what needs to be produced in our lives.

> *These things God has revealed to us through the Spirit. For the Spirit searches everything, even the depths of God. For who knows a person's thoughts except the spirit of that person, which is in him? So also no one comprehends the thoughts of God except the Spirit of God. Now we have received not the spirit of the world, but the Spirit who is from God, that we might understand the things freely given us by God.*
> *(1 Corinthians 2:10-12)*

132 DIRT IN MY SOUL AND THE GIFT OF REPENTANCE

Our enemy has one main goal, and that is to bring us down to a lower level where condemnation finds access to our soul and we no longer find it possible to glorify our Father.

He is here to kill, steal, and destroy, and he doesn't care how he does it. His goal is destruction. For Adam and Eve, he used the tree in the midst of the garden, the one that was attractive to them. For you and me, the bait might be something different. Whatever he uses, his goal is to deceive and keep you from understanding what is happening.

A part of this so-called "dirt in your soul" is often a pain of such great measure that you think your only option is to block the pain with whatever means is at hand. The problem with blocking pain is that we quickly forget what is hindering our freedom. We fall into the trap of the enemy's deception and don't understand why our relationship with our heavenly Father is blocked. After much disaster and negative influence, we come to a place of desperation and begin to cry out for help, hoping to find answers for this blocked relationship with our Father in Heaven.

It is only the power of the Holy Spirit that can penetrate the soul and reveal things that have been buried for many years. It is when we begin to ask our heavenly Father and the Holy Spirit to reveal every speck of dirt that things begin to open up and the possibility of repentance begins to shine forth.

Repentance only comes as a gift from above, after revelation comes in and we see the hurt and wounding that has occupied our soul down through the years.

Today, dare to ask Him, to show you every speck of dirt that has affected your soul, and dare to believe that He will do so. You may not know the answer to all the complications the enemy has used in your life, but one thing is sure—the Holy Spirit does. He has delivered many souls from despair, woundedness, and destruction. And He will do it for you! Dare to believe that He will deliver your dark lonely soul from the deep pit, because His name is Faithful One!

This is why the Bible says God is light and in Him is no darkness at all. Whenever His light comes, there is a revelation, a knowing, a knowledge that passes all understanding. He brings a comprehending of the Word of God so that repentance flows and we understand our hindrances. We understand where we lack, and the darkness has got to go. Freedom invades the soul. Salvation!

This is why the enemy of our soul despises the light of the gospel. The light banishes darkness and anything that is not of Christ. The light shines in darkness and darkness comprehends it not.

133 FAITH FOR SALVATION

When the heart believes and the mouth speaks, salvation cannot fail! His Word cannot fail; it is sure and will stand the test of time. Everything around us will be shaken, but not so His Word!

Learn to depend on His Word. Learn to love it. Learn to stake your life on it, and you will find stability that you've never known before.

It is only when we speak without being convinced in our heart that we are tempted to wonder if God's Word is true. It is only when sin occupies the heart and doubt moves in that our unbelief blocks the Word of God from penetrating the motives in our heart.

> *Learn to stake your life on the Word of God, and you will find stability that you've never known before.*

Sin can be anything from simply missing the mark to open, willful violations committed against our fellow man or God. Sin stains the soul. It keeps us from believing in the completeness of our salvation. It brings doubt and unbelief and all instability.

Whether we have committed sin or the generation before us has sinned, it is vital that we come to a place where repentance is found and all sin is brought under the blood of Christ. There is only One who can reveal all motives and bring revelation of sins committed that have been removed from our conscious memory.

Today, ask for the Spirit's revelation in your soul, and when He brings it, darkness will have to leave and confession will bring the fullness of salvation. Your life will be filled with the peace that comes from Heaven.

> *For with the heart one believes and is justified, and with the mouth one confesses and is saved. For "everyone who calls on the name of the Lord will be saved." (Romans 10:10, 13)*

What gives a man "the right" to salvation? How foolish to think inheritance comes because of some religious ability through education or family status! It is our faith and our faith alone that connects us to salvation.

And if faith is our only chance of salvation, what exactly is faith? Faith is connected with trust, and trust can only come when we experience the love of Christ for ourselves.

When a person experiences the love of Christ, faith will be an automatic response because His love penetrates the heart. When a person experiences forgiveness from their heavenly Father, they will automatically also forgive those who have brought pain to them. Those who know the love and forgiveness of God have found the healing needed in order to be successful God's way—successful in loving others, successful in showing others what the heavenly Father is like.

Jesus said,

> *"You shall love the Lord your God with all your heart and with all your soul and with all your mind. This is the great and first commandment. And a second is like it: You shall love your neighbor as yourself. On these two commandments depend all the Law and the Prophets." (Matthew 22:37-40)*

If you love the Lord your God with all your heart and with all your soul and with all your mind, and your neighbor as yourself, you have met the King and you understand how He thinks! You have met the author of forgiveness and you have met the one who wiped your slate clean. For without understanding how much you have been forgiven and how much dirt has been wiped from your soul, you will never be able to do so for others.

Faith connects us directly to the heart of Christ, and we can't choose only a part of His heart for ourselves. When we accept Him in our life for who He is, every part of Him should be seen in us. We might want to think we can receive forgiveness from our heavenly Father but not be forgiving as He would be. This will never work! The more we receive from Him, the more like Him we become in every way and in how we treat those around us.

The heart of Jesus was always for everyone to be saved regardless of where they came from, because He knew forgiveness would change people from the inside out. We have all met people against whom we were tempted to think negative thoughts, but Jesus knew His forgiveness was strong enough to change any person, regardless of how twisted they were. If we prove to be followers of Christ, we will desire for all people to be saved.

And we will understand our only connection to Christ is faith, and faith is not only the ability to believe for the supernatural but also a foundation found in the fabric of love from a higher source.

For by grace you have been saved through faith. And this is not your own doing; it is the gift of God, not a result of works, so that no one may boast. (Ephesians 2:8-9)

Beloved, let us love one another, for love is from God, and whoever loves has been born of God and knows God. We love because he first loved us. (1 John 4:7, 19)

Bearing with one another and, if one has a complaint against another, forgiving each other; as the Lord has forgiven you, so you must also forgive. (Colossians 3:13)

135 THE SIMPLICITY OF BELIEVING

May the God of hope fill you with all joy and peace in believing, so that by the power of the Holy Spirit you may abound in hope. (Romans 15:13)

Have we become so educated and schooled that the simplicity of the gospel has a hard time taking us to a place where we are effective for the Kingdom?

Who are those who are able to believe the gospel and all its fullness? Who are those who comprehend the depth of hope? Isn't it those who have no ideas of how it "should" be when they hear His voice for the first time?

Oftentimes, the things that we have stacked up in our thought life, ideas that we deem right and important, are the things that keep our heavenly Father from penetrating the core of who we are. But those who have no higher purpose than hearing His voice are those who will go farther in the Kingdom. Those who have decided their own agenda is useless and must be laid down are those who become useful in the Master's work.

When we face difficulty and trial, the intention of our Father is to bring us to a place where nothing matters save our Father's voice. We see it is vital to spend our time wisely because we do not know how much longer we have. When we are young, it's easy to waste time; but when we come to the realization that we are no longer considered young, we begin to look at life in the light of eternity and use our time with more intention.

When belief takes place in a heart, faith becomes simplified and corruption looks complicated. Our Father knows how to prepare soil for seed, and He sees what is the perfect scenario for seed to be planted for an abundant crop.

> But as it is written, "Those who have never been told of him will see, and those who have never heard will understand." (Romans 15:21)

He is a Master at planting a seed at the right place at the right time. To us, it may look unplanned; but He knows perfect timing, and we can be confident that He is planning on an abundant crop.

136 THE POWER IN THE CROSS

For the word of the cross is folly to those who are perishing, but to us who are being saved it is the power of God. (1 Corinthians 1:18)

What is it about the cross that contains so much power that the Spirit of God will burst forth and miraculous resurrection power overtakes a person? When someone deliberately forsakes their own way and even their own life, the Spirit of God cannot keep silent! In this choice, the Holy Spirit sees opportunity for the Kingdom of God to prevail in that person's life. All the ideas and agendas that once were so valuable to the flesh are now forsaken and Christ gains access to the heart. In this, resurrection power is manifested!

It's sad to say, but often it takes a lifetime of learning obedience through the things we suffer. Our Father isn't so concerned about how we learn, but He's more concerned that we get it before our departure and that we use our transformation to change the lives of those around us.

Jesus made it clear that the power of sin should have no more dominion over our souls. The curse of sin has been broken and resurrection power has been made available, but we have a choice whether or not sin is given the right to reign or the cross is embraced.

To the natural man, the cross sounds foolish. The natural man would never choose the cross. It is the man who can see on the other side and finds the courage to embrace something much bigger than himself who ends up finding life and life abundantly. It is the one who has a single eye and a hearing ear, the one who makes Christ his everything, who will find the courage to embrace what the natural man could never do.

The natural man asks, Why would I choose to die? Why would I choose to forsake my own life when that's all I'm living for? When it's all about my kingdom and my glory, why would I forsake it? Why would I love those who are my enemies when I have learned to fight for myself? Why would I bless instead of curse if my blessing depends on my strength? Forsaking my own life looks miserable and undesirable when I'm only living for myself.

But those who are born of the Spirit understand their sights are set on a city much bigger than themselves. Their eyes see beyond the natural, and they believe in things that cannot be seen by the carnal man. They have learned where their strength ends is where the power of the Holy Spirit kicks in. They understand how little strength they have on their own and how much better off they are with strength from above. A divine exchange has taken place, and the power that they find in Christ goes beyond their wildest imagination.

The power in the cross is not a natural power.
It goes beyond man;
it goes beyond here and now.
And it's only found when
the natural is exchanged for the supernatural.

137 FAITH AND POWER

In this world we are taught that in order to have influence and power, we need to be educated among the best and work for a place among those who rank the highest. But in the writings of Paul, this whole concept fails to stand.

And my speech and my message were not in plausible words of wisdom, but in demonstration of the Spirit and of power, so that your faith might not rest in the wisdom of men but in the power of God. (1 Corinthians 2:4-5)

But he said to me, "My grace is sufficient for you, for my power is made perfect in weakness." Therefore I will boast all the more gladly of my weaknesses, so that the power of Christ may rest upon me. For the sake of Christ, then, I am content with weaknesses, insults, hardships, persecutions, and calamities. For when I am weak, then I am strong. (2 Corinthians 12:9-10)

The power of the gospel comes forth in weakness, insults, hardships, persecutions, and calamities. Our faith does not stand in the wisdom of man but in the power of God. God's way of influence is opposite from much that we have been taught. Paul boasted in weakness in order for the power of Christ to be manifested in his life. Boasting in weakness is not popular in our human thinking.

The world offers many things in which we are tempted to put our faith and confidence. Every day, there are hundreds if not thousands of choices that face us and test where we have put our hope and faith. But there is only One in whom our faith and confidence can rest, because He makes all the difference.

What tremendous hope this offers to the one who always came up short in performance and social status! Our heavenly Father does not see life according to popular opinion; His ways are much higher and much better. All He needs for the power of Christ to manifest is a yielded vessel.

To yield our lives to Christ, we need to have a trust in a power that cannot be seen with natural eyes. Yielding to Him is called faith, and yielding to Him is our only chance of ever operating in His power. Instead of performance, learn to be good at yielding to Him. Those who yield to Christ will never be ashamed. In yielding to Him, we will never come up short from His perspective.

The world's view of power and success causes so many to stumble. Christ says, "Only yield your life, and I will do things beyond anything you could ever imagine or think!"

That's all He's asking for. When we grasp this reality, everything in life changes—it's no longer *us,* but it's Christ and His power.

138 ENDURING WITH PATIENCE

Endurance and patience are two of the most valuable traits we Christians can learn. When life brings complications and difficulties, it will be endurance and patience that take us through to the end. Even in the fire, those who have learned to endure will be brought to a place of refinement, where the gospel is made real.

When we look at the biggest trees in a forest, we find the greatest are the ones that have had gradual growth each year have stood the test of time. So is the person who learns to endure with patience. It is not an instant growth but a growing that is established over a period of time, for he has learned to trust the Lord when times are easy and when times are difficult.

Our society prefers instant results, but in our Master's Kingdom, this is not His focus. His Kingdom demands endurance and patience.

It is the man of the flesh who desires instant results and sees no need for endurance. Those who live after the Spirit learn that faith is established through endurance and patience. Forsaking everything for His Kingdom produces a lasting fruit and establishes roots that will guarantee stability.

Therefore, since we are surrounded by so great a cloud of witnesses, let us also lay aside every weight, and sin which clings so closely, and let us run with endurance the race that is set before us, looking to Jesus, the founder and perfecter of our faith, who for the joy that was set before him endured the cross, despising the shame, and is seated at the right hand of the throne of God. Consider him who endured from sinners such hostility against himself, so that you may not grow weary or fainthearted. (Hebrews 12:1-3)

139 JUDGE YOURSELF TRULY

Whoever, therefore, eats the bread or drinks the cup of the Lord in an unworthy manner will be guilty concerning the body and blood of the Lord. Let a person examine himself, then, and so eat of the bread and drink of the cup. For anyone who eats and drinks without discerning the body eats and drinks judgment on himself. That is why many of you are weak and ill, and some have died. But if we judged ourselves truly, we would not be judged. But when we are judged by the Lord, we are disciplined so that we may not be condemned along with the world. (1 Corinthians 11:27-32)

What is it to drink "worthily" and to judge yourself "truly"? To be judged by the Lord for discipline?

This world does not understand why they do what they do; they don't know their own reactions and their own motives. Therefore, they come under condemnation and do not understand why.

Do we understand our own motives, our own reactions? Do we understand why we process life the way we do? Do we understand our own weaknesses?

May we allow God to judge our lives now so that we can understand ourselves and can partake of communion worthily.

140 AN AROMA OF CHRIST

Every day, life puts out challenges, afflictions, complications, victories, times of joy, and times of rest. Wherever we find ourselves in these, we are called as Christians to be an aroma of Christ, not allowing circumstances to determine how much of Christ can be seen in our lives.

In many of Paul's writings, he found himself up against conflict and complications, but he allowed his life to be used for the Kingdom. He was used in many places to bring breakthrough to different sects of people. He knew his life was to be spent in spreading the gospel among those who resisted it most. He was a man of strength, who knew how to stand and be effective in communicating a gospel of hope to those who were lost, even though opposition seemed to be the thing that he always got in return. Opposition and conflict seemed to be the fuel that the Holy Spirit used to give Paul direction in life.

Christ has called every Christian to be an aroma for Him among the nations, a fragrance, a light in a dark world. We are commissioned by God to be effective in how we represent the King.

We are instructed to wait on the Lord so that our strength can be renewed. He invites us to come to a place of rest rather than anxiety, learning how to wait effectively. Our King is the author of peace, and there is only one way to experience Him—through His shedding of His light in our hearts.

When we find ourselves straying from rest, it is vital that we come back to Him and begin by putting our trust in His ability, not ours! The world knows when they see a man called by God, walking in sincerity, and empowered by the King.

Today, the anxieties of life have no hold on us; His rest is effective in the one who needs it. Our master knows the one who depends on Him for everything in life. It is in rest that we find strength, and it is in strength that the aroma of Christ is visible to the unbeliever.

Learn to walk in rest for your soul, and you will reflect the One who lives in a land where there is perfect peace with no distraction.

For we are the aroma of Christ to God among those who are being saved and among those who are perishing, to one a fragrance from death to death, to the other a fragrance from life to life. (2 Corinthians 2:15-16)

141 BLINDED BY UNBELIEF

In their case the god of this world has blinded the minds of the unbelievers, to keep them from seeing the light of the gospel of the glory of Christ, who is the image of God. (2 Corinthians 4:4)

We have the power to stop the hand of God!

When we decide our thoughts are more important than the Word from our God. When we are swayed by our emotions more than by the Word of God. When we have made our own mind big and the Word of God small. When we have somehow found faith in ourselves rather than in a God who has power over the natural realm we live in. When these characterize our lives, they are signs we do not have faith and trust in our God.

We know we can't save our own soul from hell, but somehow we have convinced ourselves that we can provide for our own natural needs, when in reality our King wants to provide everything from salvation of our souls to our daily needs and provision.

How foolish to think human effort can accomplish more than the One who created mankind. It sounds silly to say and we would never say it aloud, but when we walk in unbelief and doubt, we are saying "God is not big enough to handle my problems."

In order to have faith, we must establish a foundation of trust in God. The person who comes to God must believe that He exists and that He longs to pour out His blessing on His people. We must believe that God can do more in one moment than man can accomplish in an entire lifetime of travailing.

Faith is not complicated but rather so simple that a child can understand. It is those with big minds who have come to a place of refusing to trust in Christ, refusing to have confidence in the One who paid for every sin that mankind has ever committed. It is those who leave the simplicity of faith and refuse to live their lives God's way who see faith as complicated. Faith will look complicated only when we have found a way to live without Christ at the center of everything we do.

When we understand that we have the power to speak to our own minds and tell ourselves not to block the Word of God, not to argue against the power of the gospel—this is where true hope is found!

Faith in Christ is our only chance for salvation, and the one who finds salvation understands the Lord's hand is able to save. What if we start using that same faith for provision, for healing, for every need that faces us? It is no more complicated for God to provide our everyday needs than it is for God to bring salvation to our souls!

For God, who said, "Let light shine out of darkness," has shone in our hearts to give the light of the knowledge of the glory of God in the face of Jesus Christ. (2 Corinthians 4:6)

142 HIS SUFFICIENCY

How many of the battles and struggles we face come because we have no confidence in our God?

We are easily led to think our supply comes from people, whether the provision is for emotional, spiritual, or physical needs. The problem is that people will always let us down and can never be the source of our supply.

There is only One who can supply every need of mankind and that is why our confidence must be in God rather than man!

And my God will supply every need of yours according to his riches in glory in Christ Jesus. (Philippians 4:19)

God never intended for us to depend on our fellow man as the Source. God does use people as channels to reach others and touch those in need, but the moment we think people are the Source, we come into many unnecessary hurts and difficulties that could have been avoided had we recognized God as our Source of all.

143 CHRIST MY IDENTITY

There is tremendous opportunity when we come to Christ and lay our lives at the cross to be used wherever God would choose to use us. When we open our lives up to Christ and allow Him to take us where He wants us to go, the possibilities are endless. In biblical accounts, we see that those who came to Christ and lost their own life for the gospel were those who were most effective and brought a change in the lives of many others.

God needs a vessel who has no personal agenda outside of Christ and His Kingdom, one who has died a thousand deaths in order for the gospel to reach a lost society, who has no other vision but to be used in the Master's hand, who finds himself thinking thoughts toward God all the day.

We can be so consumed by our own thoughts, our own visions, and our own goals. What makes a person instead think thoughts toward his Master all the day? What makes one desire nothing else but to spend time in the Word and in the prayer closet?

It is the knowledge that without Christ we can do nothing and with Christ we can do all things. It is knowing that there is no identity worth living for outside of Christ. It is knowing what He has done for the one who was lost in a pit of despair, overwhelmed by destructive thought patterns, with no way out—but today is redeemed and has found the Source of life. Today, that person has found confidence in salvation, and their life does not look anything close to what it used to be. Today, they have chosen to put their confidence in Christ and have learned that God is the Source. Old thought patterns have vanished and new life springs forth. This is a work that can only be found in

Christ through the power of the Holy Spirit and nothing in life can ever be a substitute.

Only when our eyes are fixed on Him all the day and our innermost desire is to please Him will we find our relationship with Him becomes effective enough to make a difference to those around us.

144 GOD'S VOICE IN A THOUGHT

How does God speak to His people? Isn't it a thought from the Spirit that He brings to your mind?

When we learn to hear His voice, we know what it is to hear from God's Word. When we recognize who spoke and we act on it, Christ is glorified.

Those who are effective for Christ and have an impact in life have learned to silence their own thoughts and listen to His voice. We oftentimes miss the voice of God because we think our own thoughts are more important than the thought that comes from the Spirit. Understanding the difference between our thoughts and God's thoughts is the whole sum of hearing His voice.

When we value our own thoughts more than the thoughts of God, we can no longer hear clearly the voice of God. My thoughts can never take the place of God's thoughts because His Word says,

> *"For as the heavens are higher than the earth, so are my ways higher than your ways and my thoughts than your thoughts." (Isaiah 55:9)*

We can also miss the voice of God when our minds become noisy and life comes at us with its high demands. Be careful! It is often in the busyness of life that the voice of God takes second place to our own agendas and we can no longer hear the way we were designed to hear.

Our world trains us not only in busyness but also in instant results. God's Word tells us to wait on the Lord so that our strength can be renewed. Waiting looks foolish to the natural man, because he could be moving forward and accomplishing what he thinks is important in life. But when we wait on our God, we begin to understand what matters in life and how He can accomplish way beyond anything we could ever come up with. Waiting on Him is where His voice is detected!

They who wait for the LORD shall renew their strength; they shall mount up with wings like eagles; they shall run and not be weary; they shall walk and not faint. (Isaiah 40:31)

This is a promise to live beyond the natural—to walk and not faint, to run and not be weary, to find a place of renewed strength that no natural thought could ever lead you to!

Learn to wait for the Lord and hear His voice, and you will be rewarded for eternities to come. His thoughts are higher; His ways are better. His voice contains the power to change any situation or trap we find ourselves in. Learn to listen to His thoughts above your own, and you will know what His voice sounds like.

He knows your ways, He knows your thoughts, He knows the battles you face every day, and He says, "My thoughts are good towards you. My thoughts are much higher, much better."

Learn to listen, learn to hear His voice in the form of a thought. It will take you through life and into eternity. It will take you to a land with 100 percent clarity, where no question remains, no doubt exists, and no unbelief can be found. Don't wait until you leave this planet to experience His voice. Begin now. Spend time with Him, and you will hear!

145 OPEN YOUR HEARTS FOR SALVATION

"Therefore, I tell you, her many sins have been forgiven—as her great love has shown. But whoever has been forgiven little loves little." (Luke 7:47 NIV)

Salvation is a person coming to an understanding that without Christ they are lost and will never make it. Without Christ, hell is their only possibility. Salvation can only have its full effect when we recognize how desperately we need redemption.

Everyone needs Christ, but not everyone sees their need for Him. If only all eyes could be opened to their need, we would see many people come to Christ.

Mary anointed the feet of Jesus for His burial, even though she was questioned as to why she "wasted" such expensive perfume. She saw the value of the Savior and had no intention of holding back when it came to giving Him everything she had. The one who has been forgiven much will also love much! Those who did not understand this considered themselves to be self-sufficient.

So today, how much have you been forgiven? How much sin has been removed from your past? Have you found Christ to be the one who has set you free from a life of corruption?

If we have been forgiven much, then we must come to a place where we love much. Forgiven much and loving much must always be connected. The thought of finding a bitter root in a forgiven heart doesn't make any sense—whenever forgiveness is at the core, forgiveness is what should come out.

Think about an olive. As it is pressed, is there ever a reason to expect apple juice? Or can an apple ever produce olive oil? If forgiveness has been granted and our lives are put under pressure, what should come out? If not mercy and forgiveness, then there is still a work that needs to be done in the heart! Our Master knows and understands our every weakness, but when our lives are under pressure and Christ is not what comes out, this should be a concern.

I'm always amazed at the writings from Paul that show how pressure seemed to propel him in the direction that Christ called him to. The pressures he faced produced more of Christ in him. His calling was to bring the gospel to many, and he understood the conflict that awaited him, but it did not stop him from going forth with the gospel. (See 2 Corinthians 6:1-13)

Salvation is much more than access to heaven after we die. Salvation is an overflow of who our God is, and who our God is *now*. Regardless of afflictions, calamities, hardships, beatings, imprisonments, riots, or the comfort we receive from salvation when everything is going great, Christ wants to be magnified. Christ wants us to give others a desire for more of Him.

The world doesn't need someone to tell them how to live for Christ when everything is going good, but the world does need someone to show Christ in the midst of difficulty.

146 BLINDED BY SIGHT

In today's world, as in Jesus' day, many who claim to have sight are blind, and those the world calls blind can see. For a person to be able to have sight, it seems there needs to be a natural blindness. And those who find real faith learn that God's voice is heard and not seen.

The world system captures its prisoners by sight. The thing that is appealing to the eyes is the thing that took Adam and Eve in a direction that brought the curse of sin to an entire human race. Genesis 3:6 tells us that it was when Eve "saw that the tree was good for food, and that it was a delight to the eyes," that she took of its fruit. The Scripture warns us about deception and how our enemy brings it. The serpent brought it to Adam and Eve through their eyes; and Jesus tells us that false prophets will come to God's people and try their best to get them to "look!" and be moved by what they see.

> *"Then if anyone says to you, 'Look, here is the Christ!' or 'There he is!' do not believe it. For false christs and false prophets will arise and perform great signs and wonders, so as to lead astray, if possible, even the elect." (Matthew 24:23-24)*

It is vital that we don't go by sight and that we understand faith does not come by sight but faith comes by hearing. Faith comes by hearing and hearing by the Word of God. Learn to be moved by the voice of your Master and not by sight.

Think about Saul on his way to capture Christians. When he met Christ, he lost his natural eyesight. In order to see, he was blinded. He saw Christ in the form of light and heard Christ's voice, and his natural eyesight left him for three days. This was the beginning of a new life, a life of preaching the gospel to others who thought they could see but were blind. The coming days ahead would be a difficult path for the natural man in Saul, but he found the strength to do so because he no longer walked in darkness. He had a light to shine on his path, and he did not stumble around in the dark anymore.

Those who live their lives by natural sight will never be able to see, and those who live by faith learn to hear the Shepherd's voice and become blind to the natural. Those who hear His voice will find blessings that the world cannot comprehend.

> *"My sheep hear my voice, and I know them, and they follow me. I give them eternal life, and they will never perish, and no one will snatch them out of my hand." (John 10:27-28)*

147 A NEW NAME

"'He who has an ear, let him hear what the Spirit says to the churches. To the one who conquers I will give some of the hidden manna, and I will give him a white stone, with a new name written on the stone that no one knows except the one who receives it.'"
(Revelation 2:17)

Christ is in the business of changing lives and destroying old identities and thought patterns that come with bondage and baggage. One of the most intense battles we face after salvation is when our enemy tries to bring back those old identities and thought patterns.

Thus, one of our greatest victories is when we children of God come to a place where we understand that we have been given a new name and we stand firm in it. Old things have passed away; behold! all things have become new!

Do we understand the depth of being given a new name? It's a new identity!

When a new name has been given, our enemy's old labels vanish, and defeat can no longer hold back we who have overcome. The things that used to hold us back lose their power, and faith is heard, by His Word. Identity is how we see ourselves, but faith is how we hear His Word. Our enemy tries to bring us back to seeing our old life as our identity, but the Word of Christ comes to us through ears that can hear.

His redemption will blind us to our old lives so that we can hear His voice and have our sight restored to a new sight. Just as Saul was blinded on his way to bring destruction to the Christians in his day, so we need to be blinded to our old lives. Many who claim to see today have never been made blind so that true vision brings transformation.

Today, ask Him for ears to hear and ask Him for a white stone with a new name. He will give you the strength to conquer; He will give you a name that no one knows but you. He will use you as a vessel that contains the glory that Jesus had with His Father when He walked on this earth.

148 WALKING IN HIS KINGDOM

No matter how small the seed we scatter and how useless it seems to keep sowing, never underestimate a seed sown in righteousness.

In Mark 4:27, the seed that was sown begins to grow, even though the sower can't explain how. Sowing the seed in the right soil will produce things that you are not able to explain. When the conditions are right, seed produces and reproduces without any effort. It's the way it has been designed by our Father in Heaven, regardless if we believe in it or not. It might take faith to sow a seed, but it takes no faith for the seed to grow when put in the right soil condition.

Don't let failure to sow a seed bring regret to your life but take the time to sow the seeds needed to produce the harvest you want. The farmer who refuses to sow will soon face a famine too severe to overcome; if only he had taken a fraction of his former harvest and put it back in the field, understanding it will produce much more than he ever gained by foolishly clinging to his own harvest. The whole point in sowing is that we believe our Father in Heaven can produce more than we could ever come up with, and we understand the seeds we have are a blessing from above.

Are we sowing the seeds for the harvest we want to reap?

Seeds come in many forms. A seed can be words spoken to those around us or words prayed back to Heaven. Seeds can be generosity to those in need, or seeds of mercy by refusing to hear negative words against a fellow soldier. Seeds of sacrifice include giving my time when seeing someone who needs help. We can sow seeds by laying down our own agenda for someone else who has a hard path to walk, by thinking more highly of our fellow man, by showing compassion to those who are less fortunate, and by choosing to lay aside my life and hold someone else higher. We sow seeds by the atmosphere we carry with us as we come in contact with other people.

Seeds we sow will produce a harvest of their own kind.

It is interesting that in Matthew 25, Jesus said that those welcomed into the Kingdom asked, "Lord, when did we see you hungry and feed you, or thirsty and give you a drink?" It seems they were unaware of the seeds they were sowing. But this did not keep them from growing a harvest!

It may look like your seed is not producing, but remember, some seed takes longer to germinate. Germination varies based on seed, soil, and water.

Therefore be patient, brethren, until the coming of the Lord. See how the farmer waits for the precious fruit of the earth, waiting patiently for it until it receives the early and late rain. (James 5:7)

This has been ordained by the Creator:
Seed sown brings a harvest!

Made in the USA
Columbia, SC
07 January 2025

49794781R00126